CASTE, RACE, and POLITICS

CASTE, RACE, and POLITICS

*A COMPARATIVE STUDY OF
INDIA AND THE UNITED STATES*

by   Sidney Verba,
     Bashiruddin Ahmed, and Anil Bhatt

SAGE PUBLICATIONS / *Beverly Hills · London*

 For information address:
SAGE PUBLICATIONS, INC.
275 South Beverly Drive
Beverly Hills, California 90212

Printed in the United States of America
International Standard Book Number 0-8039-0118-6
Library of Congress Catalog Card No. 78-154207

First Printing

PREFACE

This book should please everyone or displease everyone. It
attempts to be almost all of the various things that we are told
social science ought to be: it is relevant to a current important
political problem; it deals with a more general theoretical problem;
it is systematic; it is comparative. The current problem to which it
is relevant is the political involvement and behavior of two
severely deprived groups—Harijans (untouchables) in India and
Blacks in the United States. The more general problem of
theoretical importance has to do with the relationship between
political, socioeconomic, and ascriptive stratification systems; and,
in particular, with the way in which those citizens who are low on
some ascriptive hierarchy can use the political system to improve
their socioeconomic position. The book is based on systematic
data collected in sample surveys in India and the United States.
And, of course, it is comparative across the two nations.

By being all of these prestigious things, it may be none of them
fully adequately. In comparing Blacks with Harijans, we probably
give less attention to the rich complexity of the situation of each

of the groups; we should pay more attention to internal differences among Blacks and among Harijans. Our concern with the more general problem of the relationship among stratification hierarchies focuses our attention on certain aspects of the positions of these two groups, again leading us to underplay other important features of their situations. Conversely, the focus of the book on these two groups—rather than on stratification systems in general—may raise some problems as to the extent to which we can generalize beyond our groups to our more general concerns. The data are systematic, based on interviews with samples in each of the nations; and that allows us to compare more closely and to make statements about amounts and about relations among variables not possible otherwise. But it means that we talk about huge, complex populations on the basis of small samples, and that we are faced with all the many limitations of the interview and the survey as a research technique. And the use of systematic data in a comparative context raises all kinds of issues as to the comparability of data gathered under circumstances as diverse as those in the two countries we study.

But the task is interesting enough so that we will risk landing on none of the various stools we have set out. The data offer some fascinating comparisions and allow for some comparative statements that have, as far as we can tell, not been possible with other sources of information. The wary reader will keep in mind the fact that we are characterizing vast and complex populations on the basis of relatively small samples. Where possible, we have compared our findings to those based on more reliable data sets such as the Census, and have in most cases been encouraged by what we have found.

The data come from a larger study of participation in several nations, but the Black-Harijan comparison struck as one very good place to begin our analyses of the larger study. The comparison is a "natural" one; it makes for a meaningful first cut into our complex data; and it allows us to test out ideas for further, more general analysis. It also allows us to deal with the most general methodological problem with which we are faced in comparative work of this sort: how to compare across societies, which requires abstracting particular aspects for comparison, without ignoring and thereby distorting the context from which the abstraction takes place. The book, then, is a fifth thing—an exercise in the comparative method.

The data for this monograph come from a larger cross-national study of political and social change conducted in India and the United States, as well as in Austria, Japan, and Nigeria (and, in the future, in the Netherlands and Yugoslavia). The study in India was conducted by the Centre for the Study of Developing Societies, New Delhi, under the direction of Rajni Kothari and Bashiruddin Ahmed. The study in the United States was under the auspices of the Institute of Political Studies, Stanford University, and the Institute for International Studies and the Survey Research Center, the University of California at Berkeley, under the direction of Sidney Verba, Robert Somers, and Norman Nie. Interviewing in the United States was conducted by the National Opinion Research Center of the University of Chicago.

Caste, Race, and Politics draws heavily on the data from this study and on the conceptualizations and ideas that have become the common property of the collaborators in this large, complicated and long-term study. Thus the collaborators listed above have added to this volume in ways that go beyond the usual advice one receives in writing a book. In addition, participants in the research program from the other countries made substantial contributions to the present work through their participation in the overall framework and design of the study. In particular we would like to mention Ulf Himmelstrand of the University of Uppsala and Albert Imohiosen of the University of Lagos (both formerly of the University of Ibadan), and Hajime Ikeuchi of the University of Tokyo and Ichiro Miyake of the University of Kyoto. Charles Y. Glock was very helpful on the U.S. study. Gabriel Almond played the key role in inspiring the study from the beginning.

Jae-On Kim of the University of Iowa contributed his statistical and substantive knowledge, as well as his great patience to the data analysis. Norman Nie was most helpful at various points. And for uncountable services we must mention Saleha Ahmed, Arlee Ellis, and Shirley Saldanha.

The field work in India was supported by the Ford Foundation and that in the United States by the Carnegie Corporation of New York; to both we are grateful.

Further analyses of these data—dealing with the individual countries as well as with comparative problems—will appear in future publications of this research program.

—S.V., B.A., and A.B.
Chicago and New Delhi

CONTENTS

LIST OF FIGURES

LIST OF TABLES

CASTE, RACE, and POLITICS

Chapter I

DEPRIVED GROUPS AND POLITICAL BEHAVIOR:
GENERAL CONSIDERATIONS

This volume compares the political behavior and political orientations of two deprived groups in two different societies—Blacks in the United States and Harijans (Untouchables) in India. Our major concern will be with the way in which these groups take part in the political life of their societies and the way in which political activity is used to deal with the problems of social and economic deprivation. The two groups are most interesting to compare. They are similar in many ways, the most important for our purposes being the fact that they both occupy the lowest positions on the status hierarchies in their societies and are particularly singled out from other groups on the basis of ascriptive characteristics. And both groups have undergone recent political awakening. On the other hand, they differ in many ways, perhaps the most important of which is the fact that they occupy their low positions in quite different societies. The similarity has led to various attempts to compare them (for instance, Berreman,

1960; Myrdal, 1944; Rudolph and Rudolph, 1967; de Reuck and
Knight, 1967; de Vos and Wagatsuma, 1967; Cash, 1954; Dollard,
1957; Isaacs, 1964). Our study differs from most of these in that
we are interested in political behavior and that we shall make
many of the comparisons on the basis of some parallel data on
social position and politics gathered in the two countries.*

---

*The data to be reported come from a cross-cultural study of political
change and political participation conducted in four countries—India, Japan,
Nigeria, and the United States. The field work for the first three countries
was supported by the Ford Foundation; the field work in the United States,
by the Carnegie Corporation of New York. The data to be reported in this
monograph come from the studies in India and the United States. The former
study was conducted by the Centre for the Study of Developing Societies,
New Delhi, under the direction of Rajni Kothari and Bashiruddin Ahmed; the
latter was conducted by the National Opinion Research Center, the
University of Chicago for the Institute of Political Studies, Stanford
University and the Institute of International Studies and Survey Research
Center, the University of California (Berkeley) under the direction of Sidney
Verba, Robert Somers, and Norman Nie. Further analyses of these data and
more detailed descriptions of the data will appear in future publications of
this research program.

For the purposes of this book, a few points should be noted: the studies
were conducted from late 1966 to early 1967. In the United States, the
sample is representative of the country as a whole; in India, the sample is
drawn from four states—West Bengal, U.P., Andhra Pradesh, and Gujarat. In
the United States, there were 2,549 interviews, of which 261 were with
Blacks and 2,260 with whites. The few miscellaneous interviews have been
eliminated from the following analysis. In India there were 2,637 interviews
in all, of which 351 were with Harijans and 1,779 with caste-Hindus. Muslims
and others have been eliminated from the following analysis. The latter point
is important. When we present data for the "total" sample in the following
chapters, it is really for Hindu India (and, of course, for the four states
covered; further details about the sampling procedures are in the Appendix,
and further analyses will be included in future publications of the research
program).

Harijans, as the term is used in this monograph includes members of those
caste groups defined as Scheduled Castes in the Indian Census list.
Respondents were asked to name their caste group, and interviewers probed
for relevant subcastes. Thus the designation, Harijan, includes such groups as
Chamars, Bhangis, and Dheds who are listed as Scheduled Castes by the
Census.

The focus in the book will be upon these two groups and on the similarities and differences in the ways in which they become involved in politics. But we hope the book will be relevant to two broader concerns: one methodological, and the other substantive. The general substantive concern is with the question of the ways in which deprived groups—particularly deprived groups for whom the basis of deprivation is some ascriptive characteristic—use political means to overcome their deprivation. We shall be concerned with the ways in which the political strategies they use are conditioned by certain characteristics of the groups and of the social context within which they operate. Our data will be limited to Blacks and Harijans, but the types of considerations ought to be applicable to other groups as well.

Our methodological concern has to do with the general problem of comparison across cultures. The major characteristic that makes the Black-Harijan comparison substantively intriguing—the fact they occupy similar positions in quite dissimilar societies—makes the comparison methodologically intriguing, but also complex. Can one make meaningful comparisons across societies as diverse? Before turning to a further explication of our substantive concerns, let us look at this methodological question a bit more closely.

There are several not-too-fruitful ways in which the problem of comparability can be raised. One such involves a terminological debate—ought one to use the term "caste" to apply to Blacks or the term "caste system" to apply to the relations between the races in the United States? Some scholars (probably more often students of American society) who think one can, do (Myrdal, 1944; Dollard, 1957; Cash, 1954; but also, as Indianists, Berreman, 1960, 1967; and Bailey, 1959); while others probably more often Indianists (Cox, 1945; Dumont, 1961; Leach, 1960; Dumont and Pocock, 1957) think one ought not to. The answer one gives often depends on the definition of caste one uses, not primarily on the substantive value of such comparisons.

More substantive is the concern with whether Blacks and Harijans are similar or different. Those who want to compare them often stress similarities (status determined by birth, endogamy, sexual taboos, and exploitation); those who do not, stress differences (the basis of Harijan status in the Hindu religion, the equalitarian ethic in the United States, the prescribed occupations for Harijans). And, of course, to take the debate one step further, those who opt for similarity argue that the differences cited are not *all that* different (the position of Blacks has often been justified on the basis of religious doctrine; the American creed is not that equalitarian; there are traditional Black occupations), while those opting for differences turn the tables by arguing that the similarities are not *all that* similar (the possibilities and means of circumventing birth status and marriage rules differ in the two cases).

The way out of the debate, of course, is to accept the position on both sides. The groups are in some ways similar (which makes comparison possible) and in other ways different (which makes comparison interesting). And, of course, how they are similar and different depends heavily on what ·characteristics one selects for comparison, which in turn depends on one's research question. The question of whether the groups are similar or different ought to be replaced by the question: are there variables or attributes that can be used to characterize the two groups—their degree of social exclusion, the ritual basis of their status, or what—that are relevant to the problem at hand? The result is neither total similarity nor total dissimilarity. The groups will be comparable if they are characterized by the same variables and attributes. The values of the groups on the variables and their categories on the attributes may differ or be similar, as may the relation among the variables and attributes. These differences then become the substance of comparison.

The last unfruitful way in which the question of comparability can be raised is to ask simply, "Can the groups be compared?" As suggested in the previous paragraph, anything can be compared with anything. The issue is whether the comparison is fruitful. We hope to demonstrate the fruitfulness of such a comparison.

We shall shortly consider some of the attributes and variables that we believe affect the political behavior of the two groups and see how similar or different the groups are on these characteristics. For the moment, let us simply consider the combination of characteristics that poses the intriguing complexities of comparison—the facts that each group is at the bottom of the social hierarchy in its society, but that the hierarchies are different.

Blacks and Harijans are similar to each other largely in being distinctive groups that occupy a similar position in their respective societies—the bottom of the socioeconomic hierarchy. On the average, they have less education, lower-status jobs, and lower income than the "dominant" groups—whites and caste-Hindus. More important, each group is singled out by a set of social norms and social institutions that ascribes to it by birth a particularly low status. It is just this characteristic—whereby achieved economic advancement does not eliminate the ascribed racial status—that makes the current position of Black Americans different from that of white immigrants. And Black Americans live, in their relations with white America, under many of the conditions associated with the caste position of Harijans—formal and informal barriers against intermarriage and many other forms of social interaction; stylized modes of interaction that reaffirm the status inequalities; formal and informal barriers that limit the groups to traditional occupations, and so forth. The similar position of the two groups—they are at the bottom of the status hierarchy on almost all criteria and are singled out by custom as holding that position for ascriptive reasons—makes the groups' political behavior particularly interesting to study for two reasons: in the first place, the two groups are similar in that each should have objective interests as a group that differentiates it from others in its society, and, secondly, the particular nature of their status may lead to a preference for certain political strategies rather than others.

But the similarities of the groups go further. They are not only similar in being traditionally at the bottom of the heap, but both groups are moving more and more into situations where that position is being challenged. As Harijans move from rural areas to urban areas, or, as is more frequent, as American Blacks move from the rural south to the northern cities, they move from settings in which the traditional status is relatively entrenched to settings in which this status is less clearly established. As we all know, this is not a movement from deprivation to utopia, but it is a move with potentially important implications for political behavior and social position.

We must, however, consider differences also. Though both groups are at the bottoms of their respective social hierarchies, the hierarchies are different. The position of the American Black depends more heavily on racial characteristics, that of the Harijans on a system of religious beliefs (though both those statements would have to be carefully qualified, and neither represents an absolute difference between the two societies). The ritual statuses of the two groups differ, the patterns of interdependencies between the deprived groups and the rest of society differ, the opportunities for mobility out of the groups differ, and they differ in many other respects. In India, the Harijans are the lowest in the caste system and are distinguished from other groups, but the society is stratified into a multiplicity of caste groupings. In the United States—despite the failure of the melting pot to eliminate distinctions of birth and social origin—the situation is a much more dichotomous one. Perhaps most important from our point of view is the fact that the United States and India are quite far apart in terms of level of social and economic development—in degree of urbanization, affluence, industrialization, and so forth. The hierarchy at whose bottom the Harijan rests has a distribution substantially lower than that in the United States. The Harijan, at the bottom of the Indian hierarchy in terms of income or education, is in an absolute position quite below the average American Black. In short, Harijans and Blacks may, in some sense, have the same relative positions in their societies, but the societies are quite different, and the similarity of relative position may still imply quite different life circumstances.

The similarities and differences between the two groups and the two societies suggest some ways in which comparison can most fruitfully proceed. We must be sensitive to both relative and absolute position. The most important justification for comparing Harijans and Blacks is that they occupy similar relative positions in their respective societies. Therefore, the most important comparison is not the direct one between Blacks and Harijans, but the comparison of their relative positions vis-à-vis the dominant groups in their own socieites. Do the two lower groups differ from the dominant groups in their respective societies in the same way and to the same extent? And are these differences affected in the same way by the within-nation context—for instance, are Harijans and Blacks more like the dominant groups in less traditional settings, in urban areas rather than rural areas, in the northern United States rather than in the South? But the differences between the two societies in absolute levels of development suggest that we must be sensitive to that as well. If Harijans are found to be quite similar to Blacks in terms, say, of their relative educational position (the ratio of Harijan to caste-Hindu educational attainment is the same as the ratio of Black to white), it still may make a significant difference in the political behavior and attitudes of the two deprived groups that the absolute level of Black education is much higher than that of the Harijans.

Let us now spell out our main substantive concern—how deprived groups participate in politics—and then return to a consideration of how such participation might be conditioned by both the relative and absolute positions of the groups in their society. That will in turn set the stage for the presentation of our data.

POLITICAL ACTION AND DEPRIVATION

We are concerned with the way in which deprived groups use politics to attempt to overcome their deprivation. We might begin such a consideration by asking why deprived groups turn to politics and attempt to answer that question by considering another area of combined similarity and difference between Blacks and Harijans: the role of dominant belief systems in relation to the justifications of the lowly positions of the two groups. Many have argued that the role of dominant belief systems represents a major difference between the positions of Blacks and Harijans: the deprived status of the former goes against a general equalitarian American Creed, while that of the latter accords with a belief system supportive of hierarchy. As Louis Dumont (1961: 30) puts it:

> The Indian system is a coherent social system based on the principle of inequality, while in America the "color bar" contradicts the equalitarian system in which it occurs and of which it is a kind of disease.

The distinction is certainly real, especially from the point of view of dominant ideology. Yet the distinction needs qualification. The deprived condition of the Blacks in America has often found justification in belief systems consistent with their lowly position, whether these belief systems come from scripture or from pseudogenetics. And even where the American Creed is most egalitarian, it tends to involve a belief that anyone should be able to move to any social position that his talents and efforts allow. When this laissez faire notion is coupled with a belief that individuals *can* indeed so move—that the society is as open as the ideology would have it—the egalitarian creed can function as a justification for the deprived position of Blacks (see, Schuman, 1969). It is *their* fault if they are in such positions; perhaps they did not try hard enough. In this way, quite different ideologies—the Indian belief in a static hierarchy and the American belief in fluid social mobility—can be used to justify the deprived statuses of Harijans and Blacks.

Furthermore, one important way in which the situations in India and the United States are not as different as the dominant ideologies might suggest is particularly relevant to our concern with the role of politics. There exists in each nation a gap between the dominant *political* ideology which is equalitarian and the reality of caste or race relations (see Berreman, 1967: 318-322). The explicit *political* ideology in India as in the United States—in many respects an ideology put into practice through the mechanism of universal suffrage—is one of equality. This gap between political norms and social reality is most crucial in connection with the role that political participation may play for deprived groups. Because the formal ideology in relation to political life may be more equalitarian than in other spheres and because the public nature of political life may mean that there is more pressure in politics for congruence between formal equality and actual equality, deprived groups may find more openness in the political system than in the economic or social systems. The question becomes, then, one of the extent to which they can effectively use the political system.

How can groups such as Blacks and Harijans use the political process to reduce their level of deprivation? The ways in which they participate and the reasons why they participate are the key.

Political participation may have many goals. It may be an instrumental act aimed at influencing some governmental policy or decision or affecting who is elected to some office. Or participation may be valued in and of itself—as an act that per se confers dignity or full citizenship. For deprived groups such as Blacks or Harijans, the symbolic gratification of participation is likely to be important as a token—and the double meaning of the word is intended here—of their citizenship in the society. But for groups as socially and economically deprived as the two with which we are dealing, politics is likely to be relevant only if it can lead to payoffs in terms of some amelioration of their social and economic position—that is, political mechanisms should have some effect in changing social and economic stratification hierarchies. But political mechanisms can have a paradoxical relationship to patterns of socioeconomic stratification. On the one hand, if access to political resources and political power is less hierarchically stratified than is access to economic resources or to opportunities for social mobility or to sources of social respect, political mechanisms may be used by deprived groups to gain advances in the socioeconomic sphere. This has been one of the arguments for the equalitarian consequences of political democracy. The equality of one-man-one-vote leads to equality in other respects. And in most formally democratic societies (the United States and India included) access to political resources—particularly to the vote or to opportunities to run for office—are supported by rules making this access relatively equal for all citizens. At least, formally.

On the other hand, it may be just those characteristics of social and economic deprivation that inhibit the political activity of the deprived groups and, thereby, prevent the restratification effects of political participation from taking place. This is so because political participation is voluntary. Much research has indicated that higher social status, and higher levels of income and education are conducive to higher participation rates. Thus, those most advantaged in nonpolitical ways also participate in politics more and may thereby increase their other advantages. And this situation is more severely the case if one considers political activities beyond the vote—as we shall do in this book. The more a political act requires skill or initiative or effort or resources, the

more is it likely that those whose position in the status hierarchies
is already secure will be more active.

The paradoxical relation of participation to stratification has
implication for the ways in which deprived groups take part in
politics. How can a deprived group advance in society? The
group—or rather the members of the group—may use a group-level
or subgroup-level approach. That is, the impetus may be to raise
the status of the entire collectivity—Blacks as a group or
Harijans—or the impetus may be for members of the collectivity to
improve themselves as individuals, often by moving out of and
denying membership in the group. In the United States, this would
be the contrast between the strategy of groups that stress Black
consciousness and common fate and, at the other extreme, the
"passing as white" strategy or, in general, the approaches that
would lead to improvement for individual Blacks within the
generally white economy and social structure. In India, a
group-level approach would involve, for our purposes, attempts to
improve the lot of Harijans as a collectivity; the subgroup-level
approach would involve attempts by subcastes to move ahead,
rather than by individuals. In many cases, this is done by denying
Harijan status, a strategy analogous to the "passing as white"
strategy.

In addition groups may adopt political or nonpolitical
strategies. In the latter case, advance would come by
seeking—without governmental intervention—better income,
housing, and jobs, or by attempts to attain higher social status as
in movements of low caste groups toward sanskritization (Srinivas,
1966) or of Blacks to attain respect. In the former case, the group
would first seek political power in order to use governmental
leverage to improve their social and economic position. The two
strategies are not mutually exclusive; both can be pursued at the
same time. But it is, of course, the political strategy that makes
participation vital. If a group follows a nonpolitical strategy that
does not involve governmental intervention in aiding them, they
may use a group-level or a subgroup-level approach; that is, the
orientation may be toward advancement of the individual or
subgroup, or toward the advancement of the group as a whole.
The group—organized in mutual benefit and other self-help
associations—may attempt to improve the lot of the members, or

the individual members may strive for economic success for themselves. On the other hand, the political strategy would tend to be most compatible—perhaps require—a group-level approach. Political institutions are more easily influenced by large number of people than by small, and by organized groups than by individuals.

One of the reasons why a deprived group that works through the political system to improve its lot will succeed more fully if it acts as a cohesive group was suggested earlier in the discussion of the relationship between political participation and stratification. In the "natural order of things," participation is stacked against the deprived group. Those characteristics that lead individuals to participate—awareness of politics, political efficacy, information, sense of civic obligation—tend to derive from certain high-status characteristics, particularly higher levels of education, but also income and higher-status occupations (see Nie, Powell and Prewitt, 1969; Verba and Nie, forthcoming). If the socioeconomic mechanisms that lead to participation operate, those will participate who need improvement in their status least; Blacks, Harijans, and other deprived groups will not be benefitted. To break the reinforcing cycle of upper-group participation, lower groups must substitute something else for the socioeconomic processes that lead to participation. And that something else is likely to be group self-consciousness and awareness of its particular political position. Political mobilization must be based, not on the general social characteristics that lead to activity (since the deprived groups have less of these), but on group-specific characteristics. The group therefore must assert its groupness if the political strategy is to be effective. Members of the group will then participate even if they do not have the social characteristics that would ordinarily lead to participation. Socialist parties are examples of organizations that have often been the instruments by which workers have been brought into political participation around group solidarity themes. Other group-based associations might do this as well, as might a general sense of group solidarity communicated by other means such as the mass media.

Change in one's deprived status, therefore, has different implications for the strength of group boundaries if the change comes through the workings of the economic rather than of the political system. Industrialization and economic advance tend to reduce group boundaries as individuals advance in the economic hierarchy. Political participation and political advance tend, on the other hand, to strengthen and consolidate groups. The distinction is not hard and fast. Certainly political movements can spill over into the economic arena as political demands are made for job opportunities. But, in general, the distinction seems to hold for Blacks in the United States—in the economy, the advance is individual, in politics, it is group-based. And as Sinha (1967: 103) points out for India,

> One has the impression that while industrialization tends to ignore, if not disintegrate caste, political activity tends to consolidate it.

The point is that membership in some ascriptively defined status group may simply be irrelevant to the successful workings of a modern factory; membership in a group that has some self-identity and can engage in coordinated activity is highly relevant for political success.

Thus we see that there can be alternative paths to participation. On the one hand, we have what we might call the "normal-socioeconomic-status path." In this system, status variables such as education, income, and occupation are closely related to frequency of participation, and activists tend to come disproportionately from upper-status groups. And the impact of these social statuses is mediated by subjective states such as level of interest and awareness, information about politics, efficacy, and the like. Under this system, those who need it the least participate the most.

In contrast would be the group-based participation path where the group consciousness of the deprived group cancels out their lower status and leads to higher levels of participation than would be expected from a group of that sort. Interest and awareness would also affect the level of participation, but not as intervening variables between social status and the participation measures. Groups participating on this basis would:

(a) participate more than expected, given their other social characteristics;

(b) within the group, have little relationship between activity level and status; and

(c) have a close relationship between self-consciousness and activity level.

We have not yet exhausted all the paths to participation. For those for whom participation derives from their socioeconomic status or from their group identification, subjective involvement in politics plays an important mediating role. But some may participate on much narrower grounds; they may come to participate because of a desire to influence specific governmental decisions relevant to their own lives. What leads to participation in this case is not a general involvement in political matters or a sense of group identity, but a specific set of contingent problems for which the government is perceived as the relevant actor: it is the source of licenses, specific benefits, and a myriad of other narrow outputs. What is key about this path to political participation is the absence of those general political orientations usually associated with political participation. One becomes, somewhat paradoxically, a parochial participant—participating in but not involved in politics.

Lastly, some may participate in politics because they are mobilized by others. Those members of deprived groups who participate may do so because they are being manipulated by others. In such a case, the level of activity of any particular participant will be unrelated to his own level of interest or involvement in politics. The source of activity will be somewhere outside the individual. This type of participation may still lead to group benefit, even if the members of the group are not so motivated. If a leader can deliver a group's vote, he may receive in return benefits for the group, but in this case a lot depends on the leadership.

In sum, for a group whose participation derives from its socioeconomic position rather than from group consciousness, levels of participation will be related to that status and to the intervening effects of such variables as interest in politics or information about politics. For those for whom participation derives from a sense of group consciousness, socioeconomic status will make less difference in relation to frequency of participation, but such internalized characteristics as interest and information—and, above all, group consciousness—will be important. For those whose participation has more "parochial" origins and derives from a desire to have the government help in solving personal contingent problems, general political orientation, like political involvement, information, or group consciousness, will not be related to activity, but perception of the personal relevance of government will be. Lastly, if there is no relationship between subjective measure of political involvement and the frequency of participation, we can assume that the push toward participation is external to the participant; that he is, in some sense, mobilized by others. If the mobilizer were a political party, the degree of partisan attachment would be a potent predictor. The "external mobilization" model would become a "partisan mobilization" model. The alternative "paths" to participation are summed up schematically in Figure 1. Thick lines suggest a strong relationship, broken lines a weak relationship, and thin lines suggest an uncertain relationship (where the model does not specify whether there is or is not a relationship).

The sharpest differences among the models are the absence of the importance of socioeconomic variables in the group consciousness models and the absence of a direct link between subjective involvement variables and activity in the partisan mobilization model.

One of the purposes of this book will be to see how these models of paths to participation fit the participation of the four groups we are comparing. The point is important. It may be that the absolute frequency of participation in particular ways is similar between two groups, but this would give a false sense of the similarity of the groups if the social processes by which they come to participate differ.

Before we can apply these models, however, there are several other considerations to take into account and much preliminary data to report. One of the major considerations is with the question of what is meant by political activity—the last item on the causal chain in Figure 1. Most research in political participation tends to deal with all types of activity as if they were interchangeable. Or, if one differentiates among participatory acts, it is in terms of the difficulty or cost of the act. Thus, participation is either measured by a single scale (assumed to be unidimensional) or by a single mode of participation (usually the vote). This approach, however, grossly oversimplifies the situation. Participation is, in our view, not a single, undifferentiated entity. There are alternative modes of participation that differ significantly in the ways in which they relate the citizen to his government. A full explication of these differences will be found in other publications of this research program (Verba and Nie, forthcoming; Verba, Nie and Kim, 1971), but a brief discussion will be useful here.

We can sketch the four modes of participation on which we shall concentrate in order to indicate their significance:

VOTING

This is the standard political act and an important one for a variety of reasons that do not have to be repeated here. It is, on the other hand, an act somewhat different from the other political acts. For one thing, it is a relatively easy act. It is also a relatively blunt act, in that the individual has little voice in choosing what alternatives are presented to him and relatively little influence over the electoral outcome. The election deals with major social choice, not with the specific problems of the individual.

CAMPAIGN ACTIVITY

Here we refer to activity in political campaigns beyond the act of voting. This kind of act differs from voting in that it is more difficult—requires more effort and skills—and is a way in which the individual who, as voter, can have little impact on the outcome, can increase his political potency. On the other hand, it is like the vote in that it deals with major social choice among candidates.

COOPERATIVE ACTIVITY

Here we refer to activity in which the individual works with others—either informal groups or formal organizations—to deal with the problems of his community. It differs from electoral activity—either from voting or campaign activity—in that it can be on more specific issues and, thereby, more immediately relevant to the set of problems held by the individual.

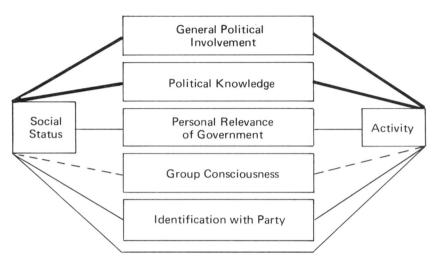

A — Normal Socioeconomic Path Model

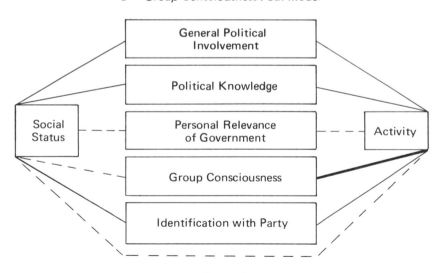

B — Group Consciousness Path Model

Figure 1

SOME HYPOTHETICAL PATHS TO PARTICIPATION

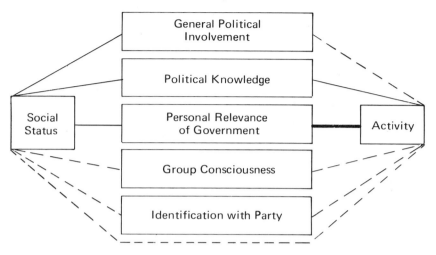

C — Parochial Participation Path Model

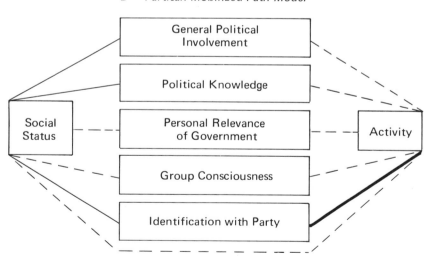

D — Partisan Mobilized Path Model

Figure 1 (continued)

SOME HYPOTHETICAL PATHS TO PARTICIPATION

CITIZEN-INITIATED CONTACTS

These are acts that differ most substantially from the vote. We refer here to contacts with governmental officials initiated by individuals. These acts are characterized by their "initiative-taking" character: the individual chooses the occasion to contact the official and, what is most important, can thereby choose the topic or the subject matter of that contact. Problems that are the subject matter of these contacts can, therefore, be highly particularized to the individual and his family. This differs from the situation in relation to the vote where the occasion for participation is presented to the individual and the subject matter of the participation—the choice of candidates or the issues of the campaign—are not set by the participant.

There is evidence—to be reported elsewhere—that these acts differ in terms of the gratifications that participants expect from them and that different types of individuals engage in these acts. In addition, the four modes of participation do appear to be empirically identifiable types of activity. A factor analysis of the various specific measures of political activity that we have used produced in both India and the United States (as well as in two other countries) clustering of political acts along the dimensions we have presented (Verba, Nie and Kim, 1971).

Thus, we have several alternative paths to participation, as well as several alternative types of participation. Let us try to tie these together by asking about the types of groups which are likely to move through particular paths to particular types of participation. That is, what type of participation are we likely to find most characteristic of say, Harijans, and through what path are they likely to move to that participation? This brings us back to the important characteristics of the deprived groups that condition their activity. Let us consider some of these characteristics of deprived groups and of the relationship between the group and the rest of society, and see how Harijans and Blacks differ or are similar. We can, in turn, then relate these characteristics to the modes of participation and the paths to participation.

Certain characteristics of the deprived group and of the relationship of the deprived group to the rest of society may be most relevant for the type of participation and the path to participation of deprived groups. We shall present data on these characteristics in Chapter III.

The Degree of Organization of the Group

Deprived groups differ in terms of their degree of internal organization: how many group members belong to formal organizations organized around their deprived status; are there leaders who can speak for them; are there internal organs of communications that link them? On this dimension, it is clear that neither of the deprived groups is fully organized, but that the Blacks are probably more organized than the Harijans. There are more Black spokesmen, more Black communications media, and more Black organizations.

The Degree of Subjective Self-Identity of the Group

Closely related to the above—both affecting it and affected by it—is *the degree of subjective self-identity of the group*. Such self-identification has clearly risen in recent years among American Blacks; and Harijans are probably over time becoming more likely to identify as Harijans rather as members of some subcaste. But it is, furthermore, quite likely that Blacks are more self-conscious. (We will present data on this.) And this is likely the case because of several other characteristics of the groups: their socioeconomic level and their degree of internal differentiation.

The Socioeconomic Levels of Harijans and Blacks

The lower the relative economic level of a social group, the more likely is the group to feel deprived and to have, therefore, the basis for motivation toward political activity. But the absolute level of deprivation is also important. Below certain levels of education, income, and the like, awareness of alternative life styles may be too low to allow the development of full self-consciousness. More important perhaps, the lower the absolute educational level, the less likely are there to be members of the group who have the organizational skills necessary to lead a social movement. It may be possible to find a few exceptional top leaders, but a large number of second-level cadres will be harder to find. In relation to this characteristic, it may be that the absolutely low level of educational attainment of Harijans makes it difficult for them to organize internally. The potential leadership base is small. And the group one is trying to organize will be harder to reach if it is generally illiterate and generally little exposed to the mass media—both because the media in general are less well developed in India and because this group in particular has minimal access to what little there is. Blacks, on the other hand, though relatively deprived in educational terms, nevertheless have a larger available cadre of educated potential leaders, are largely literate and reachable by a group-oriented press, and, of course, are exposed to the mass media—particularly television. Television is not, of course, a Black medium, but it certainly can serve the function of spreading self-consciousness. We shall present data on this as well.

The Internal Differentiation of the Group

If a group is to become self-consciously aware of its status and internally organized, a certain degree of uniformity is useful. It gives the group a set of common experiences and goals, and it diminishes internal bases of conflict. Blacks and Harijans have much in common with fellow Blacks or Harijans. They are both the lowest socioeconomic group in the society and are blocked from the upper-status groups by special social barriers. Neither group is, of course, totally homogeneous internally. The members have many different characteristics. But the type of internal differentiation is not the same for each group. Blacks are more internally differentiated than Harijans on such vertical dimensions as education, occupational status, income, and the like. Harijans tend to be more clustered in the lowest categories of these variables. Harijans, on the other hand, differ from Blacks in having much more horizontal differentiation—they speak different languages, belong to more identifiable subgroups (subcastes). In addition, they tend to be scattered much more in small villages than the Blacks, who are more in urban areas. The vertical differentiation among the Blacks does make for differences of interest, and this may impede organization and self-consciousness to some extent. On the other hand, the vertical differentiation allows for the development of leaders and followers. The differentiation of the Harijans into separate subcastes and linguistic groups and their scattering into separate small communities, on the other hand, is much more an impediment to organization and self-consciousness, since it inhibits communications and offers no basis for organizational development. Data will follow on this also.

Lastly, we can consider two characteristics of the relationship between the deprived group and the rest of the society insofar as they may affect the political strategy used.

The Distance Between the Deprived Group and the Rest of Society

The more there are barriers to interaction with other members of the society, the more likely is it that a deprived group will organize internally for political or social action (everything else, like organizational capability, being equal). Both Blacks and Harijans are in situations of high barrier. But one difference may be relevant: the Blacks are in a much more dichotomous situation. Though there is certainly internal differentiation among whites on class, ethnic, and religious grounds, the barrier between Blacks and whites differs substantially from that between other groups. In India, Harijans have some characteristics that differentiate them from all other castes, but they are nevertheless part of a larger caste system with many levels and internal differences.

The Political Channels Available to Deprived Groups

We have thus far talked of participation as if it derives from the participators; as if whether they participate and how they participate depends solely on their own characteristics. But, of course, it also depends upon the opportunities for participation offered to the group. In both India and the United States general political norms open political activity to both groups. But one difference may be the relationship to the electoral system. In the United States, there has been a long, though fading, history of discrimination against Blacks in the electoral process. In India, the electoral system expanded to cover all Indians on the basis of universal suffrage much more rapidly and completely.

SUMMATION

The above discussion leads to certain expectations about differences in the type of political activity of Harijans and Blacks. The Harijans are a distinct group with high levels of social deprivation. This provides the basis for group activity. But their low absolute level of social and economic attainment, coupled with internal differentiations that inhibit group self-consciousness, may impede those group activities that depend upon internal organization. In this sense, they are different from American Blacks who should have more potential for internally organized activity. On the other hand, the Blacks are faced with historical discrimination in relation to voting, whereas voting has been open to Harijans from the beginning; that is, from independence when voting was open for the first time on a universal basis to the caste-Hindu as well. And this may affect what they do. If some political activity characterizes Harijans, it may be voting. But they should be much less involved than Blacks in organized cooperative activity.

If we combine these considerations of mode of activity with the earlier discussion of the alternative models of mobilization, we might suggest the following expectations:

(1) If a group is ascriptively deprived but has some basis for the development of internal leadership and self-consciousness, it is likely to engage in cooperative activity and, depending upon the openness of the electoral system, in electoral activity. The model of mobilization for these activities will be the group consciousness one. Blacks, we expect, will most approximate this model.

(2) If a group is ascriptively deprived but lacks the capability for internal leadership and self-consciousness, it will be generally inactive, and this will be particularly the case in relation to cooperative activity. If it is active, it will be in acts that require little skill and competence such as voting, and the path to participation will be the external-mobilization path. There may be some small number of the group which is active for more internalized motivations. We expect Harijans to approximate this model.

(3) If a group is not severely deprived, it is likely to be active on the basis of the "normal socioeconomic model," where its activity will depend on the individual socio-economic position of the group member coupled with the level of subjective political involvement. American whites can be expected to approximate this model. Caste-Hindus, on the other hand, should approximate this model more than do Harijans. But because caste-Hindus share with Harijans some of the characteristics of severe deprivation in social and economic terms, they may participate through the external-mobilization model as well.

We have now explicated a rather complex set of relationships: particular characteristics of deprived groups and of the relationship of those groups to the broader society lead these groups to participate in particular ways and to take particular paths to participation. On the basis of this preliminary discussion, we can turn to the data comparing Blacks and Harijans. But we will not plunge directly into the complex causal models that link group characteristics to types of acts and, in turn, to paths to those acts. Rather, we shall look more systematically at the components of this overall scheme. This has two advantages: it allows us to build our argument slowly and more systematically and the data themselves that we shall report on the way to the more complex causal analysis are interesting per se.

We shall begin with a brief historical overview of the political movements among Harijans and Blacks in Chapter II. We shall make no attempt at completeness here but provide the context within which our data fall.

In Chapter III, we shall compare the Blacks and Harijans in terms of their social characteristics; comparing them both in terms of their relative positions within their own societies and their absolute positions. These comparisons are interesting per se—we do not believe that systematic data allowing such comparisons have previously been reported. But the comparisons will also be relevant to our characterizations of the two groups in terms of the important social characteristics assumed to affect modes of participation.

Chapter IV will compare the political orientations of Blacks and Harijans, in terms of relative and absolute position, to see how they differ in terms of involvement in politics, levels of information, partisan attachment, and so forth. This will give us the attitudinal basis for understanding their participation.

In Chapter V, we shall compare the groups in terms of political activity; in particular, to see if our expectations as to the kinds of activity in which they engage are borne out.

In Chapter VI, we shall relate the political orientations of the groups to their behavior in order to learn more about the nature of their participation.

In Chapter VII, we shall compare the ascriptive status hierarchy, the socioeconomic status hierarchy, and the political hierarchy.

In Chapter VIII, we shall consider the role of governmental careers. And lastly, in Chapter IX, we shall see how well our alternative paths to participation fit the participatory activities of the two groups.

The focus of the book will be on the comparison of the deprived and dominant groups in the two societies. In making this comparison, we shall engage in a minor simplification in the United States, a major one in India. In the United States, we have dropped from our sample, the few individuals who are neither white nor Black. In India, we shall drop Moslems and other religions from our sample and report data only on Hindu India. This represents a larger exclusion, and the reader ought to keep in mind the fact that we have focused only on part of India. (In the United States, we exclude less than one percent of the sample; in India, nineteen percent.) Secondly, we shall focus on the dichotomous comparison between Harijans and caste-Hindus, paying little attention to variations within the caste-Hindu group. This is, of course, a more serious oversimplification. Our justifications are that the dichotomy is meaningful; the internal variations among caste-Hindus are for our purposes less than the variation across the caste-Harijan border. Future research publications using these data will deal with the full range of caste groups.

And the dichotomy in India and the United States, though it masks complexities, is a useful simplification. Much of what we say about the differences between Harijans and caste-Hindus might refer also to the differences between scheduled tribes or backward castes in general and upper-caste groups. The process of Sanskritization, which we discuss in relation to Harijans in the next chapter, applies to other groups as well. Similarly, what is said about Blacks might apply to Chicanos or other ethnic minorities. Such questions require exploration beyond the confines of this book. The simplified distinction we make, however, highlights the relevant patterns for such exploration.

Chapter 11

BLACKS AND HARIJANS:
SOCIAL MOVEMENTS COMPARED

This chapter provides a brief historical account of the efforts made by Harijans and by Black Americans to change their conditions in the last hundred years or so. The purpose is to provide the setting for understanding the data analysis to follow. Such a comparative account is difficult because in each case the histories are complex; the movements among Harijans and Blacks contain many currents and countercurrents. And in each case the movements can only be understood in the context of the more general historical changes and events in India and the United States. The movement of Blacks to obtain equality is part of a more general history that includes the development of slavery and the plantation economy, the winning of the West, the Civil War, reconstruction, the industrialization of the North, two World Wars, the migration to northern cities, and much else. The Harijan movements are part of a history of Hinduism over many centuries, of the British in India and the Independence movement to remove them, of Gandhi, of the Congress Party, and of general economic change and development.

We cannot deal with these histories in all their complexity. Rather, we shall attempt to present a brief overview of these movements—particularly of the Harijan movement which is, we assume, less well known—and to point to some of the more salient similarities and differences between the two situations. Given the different historical settings and the differences between the two societies, there are some striking similarities in the currents and countercurrents of the two movements. Our approach will be to present a brief account of the Harijan social movements in the last century, and then to draw some distinctions and parallels with the American Black movement. Our assumption is that the history of the former group is somewhat less well known than that of the latter. This approach allows us to provide some basic information as a groundwork for comparison without rehashing the history of American Blacks.

THE MOVEMENTS FOR HARIJAN IMPROVEMENT

We can begin after the consolidation of British rule, when toward the latter half of the nineteenth century some Untouchable castes started to search for dignity and equality in different parts of the subcontinent. The establishment of the Pax Britannica, with expansion of commerce, communication, and education that followed it, was to a large extent responsible for this phenomenon. British rule opened new opportunities and provided new arenas of social life and economic activity for the Untouchables. It allowed them to acquire education and make material progress which had been largely denied them in the traditional social system of village India, in which they were not only born into the lowliest of extant statuses but also kept there, through the norms, institutions, and practices of the all-embracing caste system.

Strictly speaking, the Untouchables (whom later Gandhi was to christen Harijans—meaning God's people) were not part of the caste system, but were endogamous groups extraneous to it. The caste system proper consisted of the four *Varnas* hierarchically ranked with the Brahmin (priest) group of castes forming the top Varna, followed by the Kshatriya (warrior) castes, with the Shudras (cultivators and laborers) at the bottom. The Untouchable castes were considered to be outside the Varnas occupying the lowest positions and separated from them by notions of pollution that surrounded their position. Confined by tradition to occupations that were regarded as unclean since they involved the handling of polluting substances, physical contact with Untouchables and even their proximity was considered defiling in its effects by caste-Hindus. Consequently, the Untouchables were segregated from the rest of the community and made to live in localities of their own outside the villages. For reasons of pollution, they were barred from entering Hindu temples and denied use of public tanks and wells; they were not allowed to read Vedas (Hindu sacred texts) and were even prevented from hearing them read. Untouchables were, in fact, denied education by being barred from schools. In some areas, especially South India, even their shadow was considered to be polluting for a caste-Hindu, and, of course, nowhere were they allowed to enter caste-Hindu homes. Although they were regarded as unclean because of their occupations, they were rarely premitted to change them. Barred in most places from owning land or engaging in business (Srinivas, 1968), they derived their livelihood from occupations that kept them in abysmal poverty and complete dependence on the upper castes. Furthermore, to mark them off from the caste-Hindus, restrictions were placed on the type of dress they could wear, the ornaments they could use, the dwelling they could build, and even the names they could bear. Thus, along with educational and economic deprivation, there was humiliation and stigma that was associated with the status into which they were born and which they were not allowed to change.

Almost everywhere, the Untouchables were at the bottom of the socioreligious hierarchy; they lacked the awareness of their common deprivation and possessed no sense of affinity among themselves. Divided into caste and subcaste groupings of unequal rank based on the occupations they pursued, social interactions between them were limited by the barriers of endogamy and commensality that marked off one group of Untouchables from another. This was as much the case within the same village as it was between villages in the same district. In fact, as one moved out into larger geographical units, one found that cultural and linguistic variations tended to sharpen the differences even more.

It was not until the early decades of the twentieth century that a sense of common deprivation and of common outcaste status could emerge among the Untouchables, making it possible for them to work together for a better life, even while in most cases they retained their own narrowly defined identities. The Harijan movement in India did not, in fact, start as a movement by some Untouchables to improve the lot of all Untouchables. On the contrary, in its first phase it tended to be essentially an effort by some Untouchable castes to improve their own condition by seeking an upper-caste identity and thus denying their affinity with the other Untouchable castes in the process.

However, before pursuing this point any further, let us first turn to some of the factors that contributed to the emergence of a movement among Harijans and the forces that influenced its form and direction in its first phase. The most important of these factors was economic change that was triggered off in the nineteenth century by the British. Among other things, it enabled Untouchables to move into new occupations and roles and to gain thereby freedom from dependence on the upper castes. Construction of roads, railways, canals, and other public works started by the British absorbed Untouchables in large numbers, as did work in new factories and docks. The British also recruited them into the army and the police, while some Untouchables even found it possible to make money as contractors, merchants, and mill owners.

Change in economic roles was accompanied by educational change. The biggest effort initially to spread education among the Untouchables came from the Christian missionaries. The official British attitude on the question was, at least initially, not very helpful. The British authorities certainly did not exhibit the zeal that the Christian missionaries and later the Indian social reformers, to some extent, showed in the matter. Some of the reasons for the British attitude are perhaps best expressed in an official Minute that Montstuart Elphinstone, the Governor of Bombay, wrote in 1824 in which he argued against encouraging Untouchables in the field of education. Elphinstone observed:

> They are not only the most despised but among the least numerous of the great divisions of society, and it is to be feared that if our system of education first took root among them, it would never spread further" [Zelliott, 1969: 47].

By 'further,' Elphinstone presumably meant further among the caste-Hindus. The British did not deny education to Untouchables, but Untouchables were not admitted to government schools for fear of offending the upper castes. Instead, separate schools were established for them, as had also been done by the Christian missionaries and Indian reformers. But the number of government schools remained small in most areas. In 1882, for instance, there were only sixteen schools for Untouchables with 564 pupils in the Bombay Presidency, and four schools with 111 pupils in the neighboring Central Provinces (Nurullah and Naik, 1951: 423). Nevertheless, it was primarily the combination of official efforts with those of the Christian missionaries and the Indian reformers which enabled Untouchables to get education that had been denied to them earlier.

Important as these changes were they reached only small segments among the Untouchable castes. However, these changes were widespread enough to produce in different parts of the country groups of individuals from among whom emerged the leaders of the early Untouchable movements.

Among the other factors affecting the Untouchables, mention should be made of the machinery of revenue and police administration and of law and justice the British established throughout the country. Its most obvious importance from the point of view of the Untouchables lay in the fact that it brought into existence institutions that were not governed by the traditional norms of the caste society and were not run by the dominant castes. As such, they provided the alternative structures of authority to which Untouchables could turn for help and relief from the oppressions of the traditional system.

While the actual record of help rendered by law courts and other agencies of British Government was uneven until the turn of the century, values and beliefs underlying the institutions had the effect of corroding and weakening the ideological supports of the caste system and the practice of untouchability. The notions of the potential worth of every human being, the concepts of equality, of individual rights, of legal due process, and the like made the underprivileged aware of the injustice of their situation and conscious of their rights, while forcing particularly the growing segment of Westernized upper castes to sit up and closely examine their own society and religion. Coupled with the persistent criticism of Hindu customs and practices that came from the missionaries, who were increasingly successful in gaining converts to Christianity among the lower castes, the challenge of Western values and beliefs resulted in an outburst of religious and social reform movements in the second half of the nineteenth century (Heimsath, 1964). Reaching their peak during the 1890s, these movements, led mostly by Brahmins and other upper-caste Hindus, created the moral climate within which the Untouchables found encouragement and often tangible support for their efforts.

It was within this context that efforts among the Untouchables to change their conditions started in the latter part of the nineteenth century. By the end of the century, Untouchable castes in different parts of the country were actively working for improvement in their social status and material conditions. They were, however, working independently of each other when they were in the same region or district and were subjected to common patterns of discrimination and disabilities. The primary aim of the Untouchable castes active in this period was not protest against the caste system but assimilation within it. Everywhere castes which had made some gains from the economic and educational changes we discussed above attempted to cross the pollution barrier, as it were, by claiming a higher status within the caste system. To legitimize their claims, they engaged in the process of Sanskritization, which involved the emulation of life styles of the upper castes (Srinivas, 1968: 193). Through caste newspapers, conferences, and organizations, the need for Sanskritization was constantly stressed, and caste members were persuaded—sometimes even coerced by threat of ostracism—to adopt the dietary habits, dress, social customs, and religious practices of the twice-born castes.

To further strengthen their claims, those Untouchable castes seeking mobility within the caste system frequently turned to history and mythology for evidence of their twice-born status in the past. Their hope in doing all this was to discard their identity as Untouchables and to move upward in the caste system with the approval and consent of the upper castes and the institutions of the traditional Hindu society itself. As M. N. Srinivas (1968: 193) has pointed out,

But everywhere the locally dominant castes were antagonistic to the mobility aspirations of the low castes, and . . . used physical violence as well as economic boycott, to prevent low castes from Sanskritizing their style of life.

Thus, having failed to gain from the caste Hindus a recognition of their claims to higher status and the privileges associated with it, the Untouchables began to turn to the secular insitutions of British administration for support in achieving their aspirations (Rudolphs, 1967). Their major efforts were in the law courts, where they filed suits to gain access to temples, to wells and tanks, to roads and schools, from which they had traditionally been barred on the basis of their low status. Since the British policy at this time was one of 'noninterference' in matters of caste and religion, use of legal processes resulted only in minimal gains for Untouchables. While the courts generally tended to uphold their claims to equal treatment when these pertained to primarily secular matters such as access to roads, schools, and the like, in questions that were clearly religious, such as entry into temples, they invariably reiterated the right of the upper castes to impose restrictions or even completely exclude the Untouchables (Galanter, 1969). As could be expected, the courts' reluctance to favor the Untouchables in ritual and religious matters also extended to matters involving questions of status, with the result that claims to twice-born status made by Untouchable castes before the courts came to be consistently rejected in this period.

It was probably because of this limited success with the strategy of Sanskritization that Untouchable castes began to shift emphasis from the pursuit of twice-born status to the more mundane goals of spreading education and economic progress within their own ranks. Although these were not new goals, they really came to the forefront of Harijans' concern at the beginning of the twentieth century. But Sanskritization as an avenue of mobility was not completely abandoned by the Untouchable castes, whose interest in a higher status within the caste system survived, as later events were to show.

However, groups that had hitherto spent most of their efforts in pressing their claims for higher status turned to internal reform and programs of 'self-improvement,' and substituted an attitude of accommodation for one of claims and challenges. The spirit of this period is perhaps best reflected in the program of an organization called the *Sanmarg Badhok Nirashrit Samaj* (Depressed Class Society Showing the Right Path), which was founded in 1903 in the Bombay Province. Though established by Kisan Fagoji Bansode, a leader of the Untouchable caste of Mahars, its program was addressed to all Untouchables in the area. It urged them

> not to become Christians; to obstruct conversion; not to eat what is not to be eaten; not to drink what is not to be drunk; to spread education; to acquire citizenship; to uplift their economic conditions; to organize; to create among caste Hindus a feeling that the downtrodden should be raised up.

The program attached great importance to the removal of ignorance, "whereupon," it believed, "untouchability would also be removed" (Zelliott, 1969: 76).

This note of moderation was equally marked in a petition that another Mahar leader, Shivram Kamble, along with others, presented to the British in 1910. It began by stating:

> We the Mahar inhabitants of India, residing in Bombay Presidency, have experienced the vitalizing influence of the general awakening of our Indian people, and long to participate in the new privileges which have been granted by our illustrious Emperor and King.

It went on to read

> We do not aspire to high political privileges and positions, since we are not educationally qualified for them, but humbly seek employment in the lowest grades of the public service, in the ranks of Police Sepoys and of soldiers in the Indian Army [Zelliott, 1969: 141].

Modest expectations from the government and a concern for internal improvement thus characterized the Untouchable groups in this period. As with attempts at Sanskritization, these efforts were undertaken, by and large, by different individual caste groups. Even within the same region, caste-specific activity was the norm rather than the exception. Whether in terms of petitioning the government or of self-improvement, each group acted very much on its own. There was no sign yet of the different castes coming together into some kind of an organization which could give to their individualized demands the form of collective effort and give to their localized protests a national dimension.

Such a transformation, however, did come about during the 1920s under the impact of events and forces in the larger arena of national politics. The most important of these forces resulted from the Act of 1909, which inaugurated a period of constitutional reform in India. Although the Untouchables were not affected directly by the implementation of the act, separate representation for Muslims provided under it and the possibilities of increasing democratization of the political system inherent in it set off forces which tended to bring the independently active Untouchable castes together and to draw them as direct participants in the politics of constitutional reforms.

Recognition of Muslims as a minority whose interests needed protection against the majority opened up the possibility that other religious or caste groups might be similarly treated in the future. Increasing democratization, on the other hand, meant that the ability of a group to mobilize support both within its own ranks and among other groups would become crucial to its success in politics. As a result of these factors, the Untouchables began to receive in this period greater attention from other social and political groups and organizations than had hitherto been the case. Their importance tended to increase, particularly with the emergence of the Muslim League as a rival political formation to the Indian National Congress. In efforts to undercut the Congress' position, the Muslim leaders picked on the differences between Untouchables and caste-Hindus. The Muslim tactic was to argue that since the Untouchables were regarded by the caste-Hindus as being beyond the pale of Hinduism, their numbers should not be included in any computation of Hindu population for purposes of political and constitutional arrangements (see Singh, 1910, in Zelliott, 1969: 143).

The political implications of this argument were indeed far-reaching. If liberal and humanistic motivations had led some Hindu social reformers to concern themselves with the problems of the Untouchables in the past, the changing context provided by constitutional reforms now added a new consideration which was political (Natarajan, 1959: 17). Though the Untouchables them-selves claimed separate political identity later, the possibility of this happening gave them a political importance which was beyond their own organized strength at this time.

The Indian Social Conference had taken some steps to ameliorate the conditions of the Untouchables in the past by opening schools and hostels for them. But now the need to do more than this to win the political support of the Untouchables led some social reform leaders to organize the Untouchables and foster their cause more vigorously (Heimsath, 1964: 243-247). This period saw the establishment of the Depressed Class Mission Society of India and the institution of a yearly All India Depressed Classes Conference by these leaders. Hitherto independently active Untouchable castes were brought together under the auspices of these bodies and were provided with the conditions under which a rudimentary sense of common identity could emerge among them. Organized and led by Brahmin social reformers, the Society and the Conference, in fact, also became the first large forums for articulating the interests of the Untouchables at the national level (Zelliott, 1969: 42-46).

It was at the insistence of these bodies that the Indian National Congress, which had ignored the problems of the Untouchables thus far, passed a resolution on the question of untouchability at its 1917 session. Drafted on the basis of a resolution the All India Depressed Classes Conference had passed in 1916, the Congress' resolution, however, did not mention removing specific disabilities to which the other resolution had referred. It merely confined itself to a vague expression of the "necessity, justice and righteousness of removing all disabilities, imposed by custom upon the Depressed Classes" (Natarajan, 1959: 144). A more active phase of the Congress' espousal of the Untouchable cause, however, began with Gandhi assuming the leadership of the Congress in 1920. In the intervening period, the British had introduced more reforms. The Government of India Act of 1919 increased the representation of Indians in legislatures and extended the franchise. Though the Act fell far short of the Nationalist demands, the

> Congress and Gandhi saw the need for gaining the political support of
> the Untouchables, if only to assure their being counted as Hindus in the
> calculations for communal representation in the reformed legislatures
> [Heimsath, 1964: 252-253].

Consequently, the 1920 session of the Congress passed a resolution which, in contrast with the generalizations of the 1917 resolution, gave a specific call for admission of depressed classes to Hindu temples. The resolution, however, did not much influence those who controlled the access to temples. But the efforts of the social reformers mentioned earlier and the growing interest of the Congress the resolution reflected were both, in fact, important, because of the larger group identity and the sense of political importance they produced among the Untouchable castes. In the period that followed,

> the Untouchables' power increased as they were able to exact benefits from the Congress in return for their political support. Thus, by the end of the First World War the progress of the Untouchables . . . became a function of the political power they could exert [Heimsath, 1964].

To the process of increasing strength, organization, and political importance of the Untouchable movement, the non-Brahmin movement also contributed during this period. A movement of the middle-ranking castes in Madras and Bombay Provinces against the inordinate power of the Brahmins in social and religious life, the non-Brahmin movement had languished into inactivity around the turn of the century, to be revived as a result of the Act of 1909 and the expectation of more reforms at the end of the First World War. Intensely anti-Brahmin because it held Brahmins responsible for the perpetration of an inequitous social system, it expected further constitutional reforms to result in political domination by the Brahmins. To prevent this from happening, the middle-ranking castes in the non-Brahmin movement turned from a concern with social and religious matters to political activity and organization. In need of allies to prevent Brahmin ascendancy in politics, they brought Untouchable groups into the movement (Irschick, 1969). While the association between the two did not last long, its importance lies in the fact that it politicized the Untouchable movement by leading it toward goals that were explicitly political. It was during the 1916-1919 period that the Untouchables made their first demands for political rights and equality under the tutelage of the non-Brahmin movement.

Initially, the Untouchables opposed the reforms, as did the middle-ranking castes in the non-Brahmin movement. But when the reforms appeared inevitable, the Untouchables, like their allies, demanded separate electorates to ensure proper representation in legislatures and asked for adequate representation in government services. However, they were not given representation in the legislatures on the basis of separate electorates by the Act of 1919. Instead, the British decided to nominate Untouchables to five provincial legislatures—two of them to the Madras legislature and one each to legislatures in Bombay, Bengal, and M. P. (Zelliott, 1969: 155). In 1924, following the recommendations of the Reforms Enquiry Committee, the number of nominated Untouchables in provincial legislatures was increased slightly, and an Untouchable leader from Madras, M. C. Rajah, was nominated to the central legislature.

From 1919 onward, the interest of the Untouchables in politics increased steadily. The conviction grew among them that political rights and political power were necessary if the wrongs they had suffered were to be righted. Therefore, when in 1928 the Simon Commission visited India to evaluate the working of the Act of 1919 and to assess the need for further reforms, Depressed Class organizations were there to press their demands for political rights on their own, without help or guidance from others. Some eighteen Depressed Class organizations (Keer, 1962: 115) gave testimony before the Simon Commission, the overwhelming majority among them demanding adult suffrage, separate electorates, and full representation for their people, "who," as a deputation from Bengal pointed out,

> are unwilling any longer to depend on nomination by the government, and are tired of the lip sympathy of other parties and classes which evaporates whenever the time for practical action comes [Dolbeer, 1929: 221].

Two years later, at the first Round Table Conference in London, Dr. B. R. Ambedkar, representing the Untouchables, expressed similar sentiments when he declared,

> we feel nobody can remove our grievances as well as we can, and we cannot remove them unless we get political power in our own hands. I am afraid the Depressed classes have waited too long for time to work miracles [Keer, 1962: 151].

This new assessment of the role of politics was also reflected in the changes that Ambedkar made in his own organization, the Depressed Classes Institute, which he had established in Bombay in 1924. Gone by 1931 was the emphasis in its program on spread of education and economic uplift, and missing was the list of caste-Hindus who were invited at the time of its founding to be on the Institute's board. Instead, the Institute was declared to be "an organization of the Depressed Classes which is conducted by the members of the Depressed Classes in the interest of Depressed Classes." Emphasis on self-improvement activities was replaced by emphasis on 'propaganda,' so that the Depressed Classes "may be educated into a realization of their civic rights" (Zelliott, 1969: 125). Thus the politicization of the Untouchable movement which began during 1919 was completed by 1930-1931.

In this same period, the Untouchables also turned to the more militant technique of nonviolent direct action for gaining entry to Hindu temples and access to roads and tanks from which they had been barred traditionally. In the favorable conditions created by the increasing concern shown by social reformers and the Congress on the one hand and the growing strength of the non-Brahmin movement on the other, the first major *satyagraha* was organized at Vaikom in South India in 1924. Undertaken with the support of Gandhi, the purpose of the satyagraha was to gain the right to use a temple road for the depressed classes. The movement lasted for over one year but ended without success (Natarajan, 1959: 148). However, during the period it lasted, it received wide publicity and had the effect of producing similar movements elsewhere in the country. None of these movements succeeded either, and by the early 1930s such attempts ceased altogether, partly because the attitude of Untouchables toward Sanskritization changed and partly because success in gaining political rights opened new avenues of access to social equality for the Untouchables.

By 1932, the Untouchables had gained major political concessions in the negotiations leading to the constitutional reforms of 1935. The demands of their representatives at the two Round Table Conferences in the 1930-1931 period preceding the reforms dealt with two broad areas: political representation on the basis of separate electorates, and special privileges and protection in matters of education and government jobs. The demand for separate electorates, however, met with opposition from the Congress. The leaders of the national movement were concerned at the consequences of a separate political identity for the Untouchables implied in this demand. Gandhi declared at the Round Table Conference,

> While the Congress will always accept any solution that may be acceptable to the Hindus, the Mohammedans and the Sikhs, Congress will be no party to special reservation or special electorates for any other minorities [Zelliott, 1969: 180].

Explaining his reasons, Gandhi said,

> I can understand the claims advanced by other minorities, but the claims advanced on behalf of the Untouchables, this to me is the unkindest cut of all. It means the perpetual bar-sinister . . . . Let this committee and let the whole world know that today there is a body of Hindu reformers who are pledged to remove this blot of untouchability . . . . We do not want on our register and on our census Untouchables classified as a separate class . . . . Will Untouchables remain Untouchables in perpetuity? . . . I do not mind Untouchables, if they so desire, being converted to Islam or Christianity . . . but I cannot possibly tolerate what is in store for Hinduism if there are two divisions set forth in the villages . . . if I was the only person to resist this thing I would resist it with all my life [Zelliott, 1969: 181].

In the face of such strong opposition from Gandhi, the Round Table Conference was not able to reach an agreement on the nature of representation for the Untouchables, and the matter was, therefore, left in the hands of the British Prime Minister, Ramsay MacDonald, for decision.

In August 1932, the British Government announced the Prime Minister's decision, known as the 'Communal Award,' in which separate electorates were provided for Untouchables. This immediately led to a fast by Gandhi, who reiterated his opposition to separate electorates for Untouchables and demanded withdrawal of the Award. Since the British promptly declared that "only agreement of the communities themselves can substitute other electoral arrangements for those that Government have devised," the responsibility for whatever might happen to Gandhi now seemed to shift on to the shoulders of the leaders of the Depressed Classes. A Hindu Leaders Conference now met in Bombay to find a solution to the problem. Over a hundred caste-Hindu and Depressed Class leaders were invited to it. The conference, working with limited time as Gandhi's condition worsened steadily, finally worked out an agreement that was acceptable both to the Depressed Class and caste-Hindu leaders (Pyarelal, 1932).

The agreement, known as the Poona Pact, supplanted separate electorates by joint electorates, where Untouchables would vote along with caste-Hindus, and retained the principle of reserved seats—increasing, in fact, the number of such seats for Untouchables in provincial legislatures from 78, the number provided for by the British, to 148. Untouchables also got reserved seats in the Central Legislature, where eighteen percent of the general seats (i.e., seats not reserved for Muslims, Sikhs, and so on) were to be for them. The agreement further stated that "every endeavor shall be made to secure a fair representation of the Depressed Classes in public services," that "an adequate sum shall be earmarked for providing educational facilities" for them in every province (Pyarelal, 1932: 99-112). Since the British had already indicated their willingness to accept any agreement that the Congress and the Untouchables might arrive at on the question of the nature of representation for the latter, the Poona Pact became the basis on which the Untouchables' rights and privileges were defined in the Government of India Act of 1935.

The Conference of the Hindu leaders which worked out this pact also adopted a resolution unanimously, committing the caste-Hindus unequivocally to the abolition of discrimination against the Untouchables. The resolution declared:

> This conference resolves that henceforth, amongst Hindus, no one shall be regarded as an Untouchable by reason of his birth, and that those who have been so regarded hitherto will have the same right as other Hindus in regard to the use of public schools, public roads and all other public institutions. This right shall have statutory recognition at the first opportunity and shall be one of the earliest Acts of the Swaraj Parliament [i.e., Parliament of Free India], if it shall not have received such recognition before that time [Galanter, 1969: 136].

Thus helped by constitutional reforms, the Untouchables gained acceptance of almost all their political and social demands by 1932. In fact, so comprehensive were the concessions made in this period that when independence came it was hardly necessary to go beyond the provisions of the Poona Pact to meet the demands of the Untouchables.

Gandhi's 'epic fast,' which had led to the Poona Pact, also helped dramatize the problem of the Untouchables and produced a spurt of activity aimed at eliminating social and religious discrimination against them in different parts of the country (Jans, 1935: 11). Several temples were opened to Untouchables during this period, and temple entry legislation was introduced both in provincial and central legislatures. In some provinces, this step was supplemented by legislation against discrimination in public places (Natarajan, 1959: 169).

Gandhi himself undertook another fast for the purification of attitudes toward Untouchables and toured the country extensively for almost a year, preaching against untouchability and raising funds for programs to help improve the conditions of Untouchables. It was during this period that Gandhi started using the term 'Harijan' to refer to Untouchables and established the Harijan Sevak Sangh (Servants of Harijan Society), an organization dedicated to work for the welfare of Untouchables (Zelliott, 1969: 190).

The significant political concessions won in this period and the massive commitment to the cause of eliminating untouchability gained from the caste-Hindus, the Congress, and Gandhi, however, failed to satisfy the Harijan leaders for long. Although for a time following the 'epic fast' top leaders of the Harijans worked in close cooperation with the Congress and with the Harijan Sevak Sangh, they soon moved away to reassert a separate political and cultural identity for Harijans.

One reason for this was the absence of significant results from Gandhi's intensive efforts to open up temples for Harijans. Even some temples that were opened in the 'heat of the moment' during Gandhi's 'epic fast' did not in fact remain open for long (Nehru, 1950). A bill introduced in the Central Legislative Council in 1934 to secure temple entry rights to Harijans was defeated in circumstances that led Harijan leaders to believe that the Congress was responsible for its defeat (Ambedkar, 1945: 117-129). Legislation that did get through some of the provincial legislatures was rendered ineffective in the eyes of some Harijan leaders by Gandhi's insistence on securing the consent of the majority of temple attenders before temples could be opened to the Untouchables (Natarajan, 1959: 168). The extent of progress achieved in securing religious and social rights for the Harijans in the years since 1932, then, appeared to be too little and the pace too slow, particularly when seen in the background of the great hopes that were raised in the negotiations following Gandhi's fast on the question of separate electorates.

Dissatisfaction with change in social and religious spheres was coupled with dissatisfaction in the political sphere as individuals who had led th ? Harijan movement found that the Congress was bypassing them to create its own support base among the Untouchables. The Congress' choice of Harijan candidates for the reserved seats at the time of the 1937 elections (the first election under the Act of 1935) produced the feeling among senior Harijan leaders that the Congress was violating the spirit of the Poona Pact by nominating individuals who were incapable of representing the community's interests. If such individuals did win the elections, it was argued by some, they did so essentially with the vote of the caste-Hindus who, because of their numerical strength in the joint electorates, could invariably ensure the return of a Harijan candidate of their own choice even if he did not command the confidence of his own community (Ambedkar, 1945: 220).

Articulated initially by Dr. B. R. Ambedkar, perhaps the most prominent of the Harijan leaders (Coatman, 1933: 46), this analysis gradually won the support of other important Harijan leaders, too. Their response to the situation was twofold. In the religious and cultural sphere, they threatened to abandon Hindu religion, and in the political sphere, they revived the demand for separate electorates and decided to establish a political party, the Scheduled Caste Federation.

The idea of abandoning Hindu faith was the expression of a major change in the attitude of the Harijan toward Hindu religion and society. The signs of such a change can in retrospect be traced back to 1927 when, during the period of the temple entry satyagrahas, groups of Untouchables in different places burned the sacred Hindu Code of Law—the Manusmriti—as a gesture of defiance of orthodox Hinduism. In Delhi a conference of the Depressed Classes meeting in 1928, in fact, demanded that the Manusmriti be proscribed by the government (Zelliott, 1969: 170). These events were followed later by the suspension of the temple entry movement. Replying to a colleague seeking advice on the continuation of the major temple entry satyagraha at Nasik, Ambedkar wrote

I have no hesitation in saying that such a move would be quite uncalled for and should not merely be suspended but should be stopped altogether . . . . I would advise the Depressed Class to insist upon a complete overhauling of Hindu society and Hindu theology before they consent to become an integral part of Hindu society. I started temple entry *satyagraha* only because I felt that was the best way of energizing the Depressed Class and making them conscious of their position. As I believe I have achieved that, therefore, I have no more use for temple entry. I want the Depressed Class to concentrate their energy and resources on politics and education and I hope that they will realize the importance of both [Zelliott, 1969: 116-117].

Looked at in light of earlier attempts at Sanskritization, this new attitude amounted to a declaration on the part of the Harijans that they wanted a place in the Hindu community only on their own terms (Keer, 1962: 252). While earlier they were willing to emulate the life styles of the "clean" castes and accept their values so as to become part of the caste system, they were now demanding that Hindu society change itself. Ambedkar's major difference with Gandhi, for instance, was on the question of Chaturvarna (fourfold classification of castes). Although Gandhi was opposed to untouchability, he considered the fourfold classification to be an integral part of Hindu society (Dalton, 1967). Ambedkar, on the other hand, believed that not unless the caste system itself was repudiated would the efforts at uplift of the Untouchables have any meaning. Mere abolition of untouchability within the framework of chaturvarna, he argued, would have the effect of making Untouchables into Sudras, who, though within the fold of the caste system, were nevertheless treated as inferior to the three remaining Varnas: the Brahmins, the Kshatriyas, and the Vaisyas (Keer, 1962: 227).

However, the possibility of such a major change being wrought in Hindu society was indeed remote. And this became particularly clear now that, in spite of the commitment and support of the most influential caste-Hindu leaders, even the limited goal of gaining access to temples for Harijans could not be attained.

With little hope, then, of gaining within Hindu society the kind of dignity and self-respect they were now seeking, Harijans under the leadership of Dr. Ambedkar decided to give up Hinduism in favor of another religion. The decision was taken in 1935 at a

Conference of Untouchables of Bombay at Yeola, a town close to Nasik, which had witnessed the last of the temple entry satyagrahas. Speaking at the conference, Ambedkar drew the attention of his audience to the failure of all efforts to secure equal status in Hindu society and then went on to say:

Because we have the misfortune of calling ourselves Hindus, we are treated thus. If we were members of another faith, none would dare treat us so. Choose any religion which gives you the equality of status and treatment. We shall repair our mistake now. I had the misfortune of being born with the stigma of an Untouchable. However, it is not my fault, but I will not die a Hindu, for this is in my power [Jans, 1935: 41].

The Conference then passed a resolution formalizing Ambedkar's views. After suggesting that Harijans should not waste their energies on temple entry satyagrahas, the resolution declared:

It is this Conference's opinion that we should now make our society independent of the so-called touchable classes. The Untouchable classes ought to try to win, singlemindedly a place of equality and respect for our Community in another society in Hindusthan [Zelliott, 1969: 205].

Ambedkar's suggestion to Harijans to change their religion shocked the caste-Hindus and produced a mixed response among other Harijan leaders and groups. Once again, as in the case of the demand for separate electorates, the decision to change religion brought forth another major effort from caste-Hindus to find a solution to Harijan problems. A conference of the All India Hindu Mahasabha meeting in December 1935, at Poona, for instance, reaffirmed its resolve to eliminate untouchability. Its president, Pandit Malaviya, presented a plan at the conference under which Harijans were to be freed from the stigma of untouchability through purificatory rites to be organized on a large scale throughout the country. Pleading for time, Pandit Malaviya said, "Let the Harijans not forsake it [Hinduism] and we will apply the dust under their feet to our foreheads" (Jans, 1935: 59). In Travancore State, the enthusiastic support given to Ambedkar's statement among the Ezhavas and their subsequent resolve to leave Hinduism led to an even more dramatic response on the part of the caste-Hindus, when all temples in the Princely State of Travancore were thrown open to Untouchables (Zelliott, 1969: 210).

On his own, Ambedkar followed up the Yeola statement by efforts to win support for the idea of conversion among Harijan groups outside Bombay. With the exception of the Ezhavas in the South, support for giving up Hinduism was not very pronounced among Harijans in other parts of the country. Through the process of conferences and conventions, Ambedkar managed to change the position. Self-conscious and educated Harijans in particular became ardent supporters of the idea of conversion (Lynch, 1968: 225). But actual conversion itself did not come about until 1956, when Ambedkar embraced Buddhism and started the process of mass conversion which began first among his own caste of Mahars in Maharashtra before it spread among other Untouchable castes elsewhere. There was, however, no wholesale exodus of Untouchables to Buddhism except perhaps among the Mahars. But significant numbers of Harijans followed Ambedkar into Buddhism in at least five other states (Zelliott, 1966).

The concern with identity and assertion of separateness which had led to the Yeola declaration on religious conversion found its political expression in the establishment of a political party of the Untouchables—the Scheduled Castes Federation—in 1942.* As in the case of conversion, the initiative to establish the party came from Ambedkar. But the formal decision was taken at an All India Depressed Classes Conference which was presided over by N. Sivraj from Madras and attended by delegates representing Harijan groups in several other provinces. The founding of the party thus had a much wider support right from the start than had been the case with the move for conversion. Aside from establishing a party, the Conference also revived the demand for separate electorates—a demand which the Harijan leaders had given up during the negotiations leading to the Poona Pact. In what was the

*Scheduled Castes is an administrative term for Harijans. It was coined during the course of the 1930s when, under the Act of 1935, Harijans were provided educational benefits, job reservations, and reserved seats in legislatures. To implement these policies and constitutional provisions, the government prepared lists or schedules in which all Untouchable subcastes qualifying for the privileges were included. The term Harijan given currency to by Gandhi was considered patronizing, while the terms Untouchable or Depressed Class were considered humiliating. As against these terms, Scheduled Castes was regarded as a neutral term and therefore used in the name of the party.

last phase of political activity before India became independent, the Harijans thus reverted to a strategy of stressing their separate identity.

The Scheduled Castes Federation became a rival of the Congress Party, constantly challenging the latter's claim to represent Harijan interests. The feeling that once independence was achieved the Congress would forget the Harijans probably provided the basis for much of what Harijan leaders did in this period. In a polemic entitled *What Congress and Gandhi Have Done to the Untouchables,* published just before independence, Ambedkar expressed such a view. Once its purposes were served, the Congress, believed Ambedkar, would abandon the Harijans the way the Republicans abandoned the Negroes after the Civil War. The Scheduled Castes Federation thus devoted its efforts during the 1942-1946 period to bring pressure on the British for recognition of Harijans as a separate minority whose rights and interest required special safeguards. It wanted the British not only to recognize this, but also to take the necessary constitutional steps in this regard before withdrawing from the subcontinent. Otherwise, it believed, the Congress might ignore Harijan interests once the British left. The demands of the Scheduled Castes Federation received little attention in this period, as the situation created by the Muslim League's demand for Pakistan became an all-absorbing concern of the major actors involved in the final stages of negotiations leading to Indian independence.

The Scheduled Castes Federation's claims that it alone and not the Congress represented the Harijan community were put to the test in the 1946 elections to the provincial legislatures.* Notwithstanding all its efforts in behalf of the Harijans, it was the Congress that won an overwhelming victory in reserved constituencies. Although there is some basis for suggesting, as Ambedkar did, that the Congress won because of joint electorates where Harijan candidates set up by the Congress were returned mostly because of caste-Hindu votes. The 1946 results turned out to be a major blow to the Scheduled Castes Federation from which it was never quite able to recover.

---

*The 1946 elections were the second held under the Act of 1935, the first being held in 1937. No elections were held in the intervening period due to World War II.

With the coming of independence, the Congress Party consolidated its position among the Harijans by implementing the promises it made during 1932. Untouchability was abolished legally under Article 17 of the Constitution. Other articles in Part III of the Constitution guaranteed equality of rights and status to all citizens and protected them against any discrimination on grounds of caste, religion, and so on in the areas of education, jobs, and use of recreational and other public facilities. Article 25 provided the state with a constitutional basis for throwing open Hindu temples and other religious institutions to all members of the faith, while Article 35 gave Parliament the power to declare the practice of untouchability a cognizable offence. (It was under this provision that the Indian Parliament passed the Untouchability [Offenses] Act by a unanimous vote in April 1955.) Provision for reserved seats in the central and state legislatures was made for Harijans and special privileges and benefits in government employment and education were provided for them. To oversee and supervise the implementation of these safeguards the Office of the Commissioner for Scheduled Castes and Tribes was created (Dushkin, 1961; Galanter, 1961a). Thus, the rationale for a separate political party to protect the Harijans was, by and large, eliminated by these steps that the Congress took after independence.

From 1947 to 1951, there was, in fact, a period of cooperation between the Congress and all sections of the Harijan leadership. As a gesture of good will on the part of the Congress, Dr. Ambedkar, who had all along been critical of the Congress, was included in Nehru's cabinet as Law Minister and entrusted with the important task of drafting and piloting the Constitution through the Constituent Assembly. Other Harijan leaders were either already in the provincial cabinets or were brought in after independence. Likewise, Harijan representatives occupied important positions in the councils of state and national organizations of the Congress Party.

In 1951, however, Dr. Ambedkar left Nehru's cabinet as a result of differences with the Congress leadership over the question of reform of Hindu personal law. From 1951 until his death in 1956, Dr. Ambedkar devoted his efforts to the revival of the Harijan movement. But his efforts did not succeed, because the whole set of assumptions on which the movement had developed in the past were no longer valid. The Congress had, through both the incorporation of provisions in the constitution and such gestures as inclusion of Harijan leaders into cabinets, almost destroyed the basis for any fear that Harijan interests would not be protected. An indication of the problem Dr. Ambedkar faced, therefore, was provided by the contents of the election manifesto that the Scheduled Castes Federation published at the time of the first general elections, held under the new Constitution in 1951-1952. Except for the statement that reservations in jobs for Harijans should be made subject to minimum qualifications until adequate representation is secured by the community in the military and civil services of the country, there were no other items that could be considered as of exclusive Harijan interest. The rest of the manifesto dealt with issues of broader concern, such as birth control, cooperative farming, foreign policy, nationalization of industry, and formation of linguistic states.

In the elections themselves, the party was once again trounced, and its leader, Dr. Ambedkar, defeated by a Congress Harijan candidate. Out of the 550 seats it contested for state legislatures, the party won only 16 seats distributed over 6 state legislatures, and thus managed to remain afloat until the 1957 elections, following which it was replaced by the Republican Party (Tinker, 1962: 50). The Republican Party was conceived by Dr. Ambedkar as an alliance of Harijans, backward classes, and tribes. His expectation was that, given the combined numerical strength of these groups, such a party would succeed against the Congress where the Scheduled Castes Federation had failed. Although the Republican Party, which was formally announced after Ambedkar's death, survives today, it has fared no better than did its predecessor, the Scheduled Castes Federation.

In recent years—particularly in the 1960s—the Harijans have moved somewhat away from both the traditional mode of status mobility, Sanskritization, and away from the more radical separatist movements. Rather, the tendency has been to work through the structures and processes provided by a relatively open and competitive political system (Betteille, 1965; Lynch, 1968; Bhatt, 1969). Harijan voting, as we shall see in some detail, is a potent political force, and Harijan leaders have used these votes effectively to make political gains. In contrast, protest movements based on satyagraha and direct action have become rare and ineffective. And while groups of Harijans have rejected Hindusim and the caste system (many embracing Buddhism), there seems to be among Harijans little organized attempt to undermine the political system and little intense antagonism toward it. (In part, the reason for this may lie in the absence of a countertendency to Harijan advancement. There has not been any organized attempt on the part of Hindu-revivalist groups to reject or undermine the Harijan attempts at emancipation. Hindu-revivalist groups seem to have selected Muslims as their target.)

The main effort of Harijan leaders both within and outside of the dominant Congress party has been directed at obtaining the maximum possible benefit from various government programs. A major effort has gone into the extension of the special provisions for legislative and governmental positions and the special schemes for Scheduled Caste development. These were initially meant for a short existence, but have been extended.

On the local level, Harijan leaders have directed their efforts at bargaining with leaders of factions of the dominant party. By using the electoral strength they control, they try to obtain benefits for Harijan individuals or for the group. The Republican Party, primarily organized to create a separate political force for Harijans, sometimes works as a pressure group in the factional fights within the Congress Party or enters alliances with non-Harijan political leaders, if circumstances so demand (Bhatt, 1963; Lynch, 1968).

A similar role is played by Harijan leaders at the state and central levels. After the death of Prime Minister Shashtri, the support of the Harijan members of the Congress Party in Parliament, led by Jagjivan Ram proved decisive in electing Indira Gandhi Prime Minister. And after the recent Congress split, Jagjivan Ram occupies the position of President of the ruling Congress Party* and holds an important portfolio in the Indian cabinet. The Harijan support for the winning faction pays off; after the split, the ruling Congress Party increased the reserved quota for Harijans in government jobs.

At the present moment, at least, the electoral process and the political struggles for power within the major political groups seem to be the main arenas of activity for Harijans.

---

*Mr. Ram moved out of his position as President of the Congress Party on March 22, 1971, on the completion of an extended term as head of the party. Dr. D. Sanjivayya, another Harijan leader, has now been elected in his place.

A COMPARISON OF HARIJAN MOVEMENTS
WITH BLACK MOVEMENTS

We may now turn to a consideration of some of the similarities and differences between the movements among Harijans for social advancement and those of Blacks in the United States. The time span involved is roughly comparable, since the movements in which we are interested date largely from the latter half of the nineteenth century. As pointed out above, we shall not attempt a history of the Black movement in the United States parallel to the sketch of the Harijan movement. We assume that the former is well known and well documented in many places (two standard works are Franklin, 1969; Lomax, 1962). Rather, using the framework established in the short sketch of Harijan history, we shall point to some of the most important similarities and differences in the strategies pursued by the two groups.

In drawing these parallels we shall be engaged in what can be quite a tricky intellectual game. Later in this volume, when we consider some parallels between the social positions and political activities of these two groups, we shall be comparing roughly similar bodies of data across the two countries. Even in this case, the problem of what is equivalent across nations is most complicated. But when one is comparing historical movements, the criteria of similarity and difference and the question of what is indeed comparable become much more complicated and tenuous. If one were to sift the histories of the two movements finely enough, one could probably find an analogous event, or an analogous leader, or an analogous organization among the Blacks for every such event, leader, or organization one found among the Harijans.

However, the danger of distortion is not too great. If one looks only at the main currents of the Harijan and the Black movements and considers only the most salient events, people, and organizations, the similarity in general tendencies is quite clear. And some of the most salient differences are clear as well. Let us consider these.

Elite, Mass and Outside Support

For both the Harijans and the Blacks, much of the earlier social movements depended heavily upon a few leaders from those groups and less upon the widespread support of a mass base. The history of the two movements in the late nineteenth and early twentieth centuries tends to be a history of statements and manifestos by a few leaders or of meetings among some central figures, rather than a history of mass movements, large-scale demonstrations, or massive involvement in voting and other political activities. Thus, one has the resolution of the All India Depressed Classes Conference in 1916, or the founding of the Depressed Classes Institute by Ambedkar in 1924; or the founding of the Niagara Movement in 1905 led by W. E. B. DuBois and twenty-nine Negro intellectuals, followed shortly thereafter by the equally small meetings of the National Association for the Advancement of Colored People (NAACP).

During this early period, one also finds similarities in the dependence on groups and individuals outside the depressed groups themselves for support and sometimes for leadership. Thus, an early dependence upon Brahmin humanitarians is paralleled in the American Negro movement by the role played by white liberal leaders. The period we are considering dates roughly from about 1870, when Charles Sumner introduced the far-reaching Civil Rights Bill into Congress, and encompasses the joint founding of the NAACP in 1909 by DuBois and others of the Niagara movement and by a group of white liberals.

A most interesting parallel across the two groups in the use of outside support involves the role played by the courts. For the Harijans, the British Courts represented an external legal system uncommitted to the traditional repressive norms of the localities within which Harijans lived, and committed instead—at least in terms of general value—to universalistic values quite different from those traditional to Hinduism. Similarly, the federal courts represented for the Blacks an external legal system independent of local and state governments. As pointed out above, the British courts were reluctant to act in matters that related to traditional Hindu religious beliefs. And even where the courts did act in more secular matters, the actual enforcement of court decisions often lagged quite a bit. In the United States, the courts in the late nineteenth century were of little use to the Negro movement. In the Civil Rights cases, the Fourteenth Amendment was rendered ineffective as a protective device for the deprived group, and in *Plessy v. Ferguson* the court confirmed the separate but equal doctrine.

Nevertheless, the courts as the keepers of values external to the local community did play a major role in providing an alternative set of standards and an external institution to which the deprived groups could turn to obtain relief from the more repressive local institutions. In the United States, much of the impact of the federal courts on the civil rights movement did not come until the 1940s and the 1950s. But, in that era—starting with the cases of *Morgan v. Virginia* that made segregation in interstate trains unconstitutional, and *Shelly v. Kraemer* that barred the restrictive covenant of the 1940s to the school desegregation cases in the 1950s and 1960s—the federal courts have played a major role indeed.

The Variety of Goals

Three tendencies can be found in both the Black and the Harijan movements in terms of their overall goals:

(a) full acceptance and equality within the dominant system;
(b) amelioration of one's deprived status; and
(c) rejection of the dominant values of the system.

(a) Full equality within the system: For both Harijans and Blacks, an early and prevalent tendency was to seek equality within the dominant structure of the society. Only later, when this was frustrated, do other tendencies appear. Among the Blacks, efforts were made in the latter part of the nineteenth century to improve the educational opportunities available to them—efforts supported by religious groups such as the American Missionary Association and the Freedmen's Aid Society of the Methodist Church, often aided by northern white philanthropists. Although the educated numbered relatively few, the hope was that this might be the key to full equality. Parallel to this were the many attempts on the part of Untouchable castes to move out of Untouchable status via Sanskritization and appeals to the courts for redesignation as a non-Untouchable caste. The important similarities between these two movements lie in the attempt to mix with the mainstream of society and accept its dominant values coupled with a stress on the improvement of the individual

member or some subgroup of the deprived group rather than on improvement for the deprived group as a whole.

In relation to attempts to attain equality in the social and economic systems (largely through education and higher-status employment), one finds a sharp difference between the Blacks and the Harijans—a difference that reflects the fundamental contrast between the social structure in the United States and that in India. In the United States, social status is defined on a much more individualistic basis than in India. It is true that one of the major determinants of social status is membership in one racial group rather than in another. But within each broad grouping, status is determined relatively individualistically, and upward social mobility for Blacks—either by entering "the Black bourgeoisie" or by passing as white—could take place to a large extent on an individual or family basis. In India, in contrast, social status within either the deprived or the dominant group depends upon one's membership in some subcaste. Untouchables have been historically organized into a large number of separate caste groupings, themselves largely endogamous. The intense group basis of Indian society makes movement out of such a caste group into another largely impossible for the individual, thereby eliminating the "passing as white" strategy. Furthermore, one's dependence on one's subcaste makes the attainment of higher social status through eduction or other forms of mobility relatively unrewarding for the individual if the entire group does not move with him. Thus, in India, the main thrust of the movement to attain social and economic equality for Untouchable castes has involved an attempt at *caste* mobility—not involving Untouchables as a whole, but some subcastes. The group attempts to move upward through emulation of higher castes.

(b) The "separate but not quite equal" goal: Another parallel tendency is toward an accommodative position vis-à-vis the dominant groups. As illustrated above, the Mahars in Bombay in the early part of the twentieth century attempted improvement that was less challenging to those above them. They wanted internal self-improvement, not movement into the dominant caste group, and their aspiration was not for full equality in employment and education. Rather, they aspired to the

attainment of greater dignity and stability while remaining on lower occupational levels.

This movement is, of course, a close parallel to the accommodative philosophy of Booker T. Washington, who—to the dismay of many educated Blacks—called on his fellow deprived group members to "let down your buckets where you are." He attempted to remove the sense of anxiety among the dominant white majority by suggesting that his group did not seek full social equality but sought rather to provide services for the dominant white community. His advocacy of vocational education and of training for service was strikingly similar to the call by the leaders of the Mahar Untouchable group in 1910:

> We do not aspire to high political privileges and positions, since we are not educationally qualified for them, but humbly seek employment in the lowest grades of the public services [Zelliott, 1969: 141].

In each case, the goal was accommodation by accepting a more menial position in society, and, by assuring the dominant groups that theirs was not a challenge to the dominant position, the leaders of these accommodative movements hoped to obtain the philanthropic support of those above.

(c) The rejection of the system: Given the frustrations with the attempt to achieve social and economic equality within the dominant social and economic system, and given the frustrations of an accommodation that would keep the deprived groups permanently in that position, it is not surprising that in each case one also sees emerging a third tendency—a tendency to reject the overall system within which the deprived groups live. In India, this movement, initially led by Dr. Ambedkar, took the form of a rejection of Hinduism. Within Hindu society, he argued, the deprived condition of Untouchables was inevitable. If one wanted equal status on one's own terms, one had to withdraw from the society. The idea of conversion out of Hinduism was suggested in the mid-1930s and received enthusiastic support among several Untouchable groups—though most did not embrace the idea. Actual conversion did not take place until 1956, when Ambedkar embraced Buddhism and was followed by mass conversions among his own caste of Mahars and by conversion in a number of other states.

In America, the obvious parallels are the separatist and Black
Nationalist movements. One of the first such movements began in
the early 1920s under Marcus Garvey. Garvey agreed with Booker
T. Washington that white America was not willing to accept Blacks
on equal terms. But his solution was sharply different. One can
not rely on the good will of the whites, but rather, he taught, one
has to rely solely on the efforts of the Black. One rejected the
values of white society and accepted a separate Black value
system. And, above all, he considered that success for the
American Black could only be attained by physical withdrawal
from the American system and a return to Africa. The movement
received substantial support from a minority of American Blacks,
though it never led to the massive return of which Garvey had
dreamed. And, of course, the movement rejecting the dominant
American society has been carried on in recent times by a variety
of Black Nationalist groups, starting perhaps with the Black
Muslims, who have argued that the future of the Blacks requires a
rejection of the dominant social system and separation from white
society (Essein-Udom, 1962; Lincoln, 1961).

Direct Action

One hardly need mention the obvious parallel between the two
groups in the use of direct action. Untouchables have used such
techniques for gaining entry into Hindu temples and to roads and
wells from which they had been traditionally barred. In the United
States, this is of course paralleled by the sit-in movement for
access to similar facilities that began in the early 1960s.

There is one curious difference: those who undertook the first
major Untouchable satyagraha in South India in 1924 adopted the
technique from members of the dominant castes who, led by
Gandhi, had been using it against the British. In the United States,
this technique (which may have had some roots in India) spread in
the opposite direction—first used by Blacks in relation to racial
discrimination and then spreading to white groups involved in a
variety of political movements, but especially in protests against
the war in Vietnam.

Blacks and Harijans in the Electoral Process

A good deal of the data in the following parts of this volume will deal with the role of the two deprived groups in the electoral process—their voting behavior and their other partisan activities. But we might mention here some interesting parallels in terms of the dilemma faced by these groups in engaging in electoral activity.

In each case, the deprived group has largely linked its political fate to one political party—the Democratic party or the Congress party. Blacks attached themselves to the Democratic party during the New Deal. And since then they have voted with more cohesion than almost any other group in the United States, usually giving eighty-five percent or more of their votes to the Democratic candidate in national elections. In addition, because of their geographic concentration in certain key urban areas, their voting strength becomes significant indeed to the Democratic party. Harijans have generally given their vote to the Congress party. The Scheduled Castes Federation and its successor, the Republican party, attempted to organize Harijans into an opposition party, but these movements achieved little success. Similarly, separate Black political parties have had little impact on American politics and little support among Black voters. On the other hand, the attachment to the dominant political party may bring with it some costs as well as some benefits. In each case, the political leader from the deprived group becomes a member of a larger political organization. He is often called upon to act as a supporter of that organization rather than as a representative of radical change for his own group (Wilson, 1960). In this way, radical political leadership often moves out of the hands of the political leaders and into the hands of others.

For both Harijans and Blacks, voting strength has been used to obtain benefits from the political system. This includes: for Blacks, general legislation such as the Civil Rights Act of 1964 as well as, within localities, more equitable application of justice and better school facilities (Wilson, 1964); for Harijans, such general legislation as that having to do with reserved positions and special development plans, as well as more local benefits. In each case, the success of this depends on pressure upon but also cooperation with the dominant party groups in the society. Laws such as the Civil Rights Act or the extension of reserved seat privileges for Harijans depend upon the support of political leaders from the dominant group. Thus the voting strength is used in most cases as a more or less effective force within the mainstream of the electoral system.

One important difference between Blacks and Harijans in relation to the electoral system should be pointed out. Blacks entered American politics when there was a well-established electoral system. A major thrust of their activities has been for equal access to the system. In India, Harijans received the franchise as part of a more general change in the electoral system associated with independence from the British and the founding of the Indian nation. Thus their right to vote since independence has never been questioned.

On the other hand, serious debates have existed during this century about the possibility of separate constituencies for Harijans. Separate constituencies were rejected, but Harijans now have reserved seats in state legislatures and in the National Parliament, though both Harijans and others vote in the elections for the reserved and nonreserved seats. In the United States, separate constituencies sometimes exist as the result of de facto residential segregation patterns, but specifically reserved seats for Blacks have never been considered.

The Sequence of Events

Thus we see that many of the currents in the Harijan movement have close parallels in the Black political movement. To repeat a warning earlier, this is not to argue for identity. But it certainly argues that the similar structural position of these two groups—despite the vast differences in the two societies—may have a dominant effect in pushing them in one political direction rather than in another.

It is also interesting to consider the sequence with which various political movements arise between the two groups. It is hard to locate this sequence too precisely, since currents and counter-currents go on at the same time. Nevertheless, one senses the following pattern: early movements tended to involve nonpolitical attempts at social and economic advance within the dominant system. In a relatively unorganized way—or organized in subcastes—the deprived groups attempted to achieve the status and life style they saw among the more dominant segments of society. The severity of the deprivation and the social structural barriers to advancement doomed such attempts to failure.

One counter-movement following upon this was for accommodation. The groups gave up attempting to achieve full equality and settled for something less. However, this kind of movement, which depends upon a willingness among the members of the deprived groups permanently to accept that status, was easily challenged and replaced. It was challenged by more militant leaders, by events such as the World Wars for the United States and the independence movement for India that shattered a variety of traditional patterns, and by a growing unwillingness among the deprived group to accept the accommodation.

The next stage had several characteristics and a variety of movements going on simultaneously.

One such movement was the turn toward politics. Whether it was through the attempt to increase the potency of the group as an electoral force, or the attempt to obtain more political offices for the members of the group, or the attempt to obtain greater access to the government, political activities were seen as more and more the key to success for the deprived group.

Closely related to this tendency is a growing independence from outside leadership. Though earlier the movements often had white or Brahmin or other caste-Hindu leadership, over time the tendency is for a reduction in the role of these external groups. The earlier role of external leaders resulted from the lack of leadership within the deprived group; the reaction against this reflects the growth of trained leadership within the groups, as well as the desire to exercise fully that leadership potential.

These two tendencies are accompanied by a gradual "encapsulation" of the deprived group. It turns more inward and attempts to organize itself into a cohesive unit in order to be more effective in dealing with the rest of society. This represents, of course, the opposite pole from the first stage of the movement, where the individuals and subgroups sought equality by disassociating themselves from the deprived group and moving into the dominant group. This encapsulation seems to have gone further among Blacks, where, for a variety of reasons, self-conscious awareness of their deprived status has gone beyond that among the Harijans.

Political mobilization goes along with this encapsulation—the former both depends upon and reinforces the latter. But the groups differ somewhat here. One's impression is that the Harijans have concentrated more recently on the use of the electoral and party system, swinging their political weight so as to obtain the most benefit for themselves. Black political activity has also taken this approach, but it is an approach paralleled by a large number of other approaches, militant and nonmilitant. The political life of the American Black seems more variegated than that of the Harijan. One can find in the history of the Harijan movements parallel tendencies to most currents among Blacks—from abandonment of the system to separatist political parties to direct action. But while all these tendencies survive among Blacks, they have been replaced by the more dominant focus on electoral politics among Harijans.

We shall try to shed some light on the source of this phenomenon. Our explanation—which we shall try to support with our data—is that Harijans tend to be mobilized at the top and at the bottom. That is, there are a very few active and articulate leaders at the top, and a large available voting base at the bottom. What is missing is a middle group—a large, potentially active group, capable of being mobilized for more "intense" activities, whether that be organization-building or direct action.

SUMMATION

The parallel in the sequence of movement among Blacks and Harijans is, we must admit, apparent only if one does not look too closely. The similarities appear in broad outline, but only in broad outline. The various stages would differ substantially if examined more closely; the various movements have counter-movements and internal complexities that would immediately make it clear that any simple parallelism is too simple.

However, the similarities in broad outline are worthy of attention. It may be that the positions of deprived groups like the Blacks and the Harijans represent such a dominant force in their political life that they have little alternative in the strategies they pursue. But that in itself is a most compelling conclusion.

As pointed out earlier, this brief sketch of some parallels in the history of the Black and Harijan movements is intended as an introduction to the primary task of this book; a close examination of some parallel data on the social circumstances and political activities of the two groups. To that task we now turn.

Chapter III

BLACKS AND HARIJANS: SOCIAL
AND ECONOMIC POSITIONS COMPARED

The comparison of the social and economic positions of Harijans and Blacks immediately raises all the problems of comparison mentioned earlier. We want to compare their social and economic positions, but their positions are in quite different societies. In our samples, for instance, we find fifty-seven percent of the Indian working population engaged in agriculture; but less than ten percent of the work force in the United States is so engaged. And, of course, income distribution and the like are sharply different across the countries. From our point of view, the social and economic characteristics of the two groups are important for two reasons. In the first place, the position of the group sets the problem for which political activity may be relevant. We are interested in the use of political participation as a means of redressing socioeconomic inequalities. The data in this section will help specify the extent of those inequalities. In the second place, the socioeconomic position of a group is important because it has an impact on the amount and type of activity of that group. It is a prime independent variable for explaining participation.

In comparing Harijans and Blacks, we will want to keep in mind three types of comparisons that are relevent to our general concern. One comparison—probably the most important—is of their relative positions in the two societies. The second has to do with their absolute positions and the comparison of these across the countries. And the third has to do with the extent of their "concentration"—to what extent the members of the group are found in the same social categories.

Occupational Structure

The comparison of occupational structures across societies— especially when one society is relatively underdeveloped and agricultural and the other highly industrialized—is difficult. Different occupations exist, seemingly similar occupations are pursued differently (in one case, an occupation can be highly skilled involving complex machinery, in another a seemingly similar occupation may require little skill or training), the prestige rankings of occupations can differ, and so forth. The problem is made more complex by the fact that occupational status is itself such a complex set of statuses—one would categorize occupations differently if one were interested in prestige rankings, income rankings, skill rankings, or rankings in terms of autonomy of control over one's work environment. The data we report, therefore, will be full of ambiguity; but many of the differences are large enough to make the comparisons significant.

Tables 1 to 4 report the occupational distributions of the four groups we are studying. Occupations are classified using a modified form of the International Labor Organization's classification scheme. Across the rows of the tables, we categorize occupations by sector of the economy, and down the column by a rough set of distinctions based on the hierarchical status of the occupation.

In India, Harijans and caste-Hindus are almost equally represented in the agricultural sector—sixty-four percent of Harijans as against sixty-five percent of caste-Hindus. In America,

Table 1

OCCUPATIONAL DISTRIBUTION OF WHITE FAMILIES
(in percentages)

Occupational Level	Occupational Sectors			Total %
	Primary Sector	Manufacturing and Mining	Clerical, Sales and Service	
Unskilled laborers	Agricultural laborers	Unskilled non-agricultural laborers	Street vendors, maids, char-workers, etc.	
	2	4	1	7
Semi-skilled laborers		Laborers in mining, trans-portation, ship-ping, etc.	Launderers, cooks, building care employees, etc.	
		19	4	23
Small independent occupations	Farmers & farm managers	Self-employed repairmen, carpenters, etc.	Proprietors of wholesale and retail trade	
	8	3	4	15
Skilled occupations		Skilled workers, craftsmen, me-chanics, repair-men, construc-tion machinery operators	Firemen, police-men, guards, etc.	
		17	2	19
Clerical, sales and low tech-nical occupations			Clerical workers, salesmen, book-keepers, etc.	
			19	19
High technical, professional and managerial occupations			Technicians, man-agers, lawyers, doctors, profes-sors, engineers, etc.	
			17	17
Total %	10	43	47	100
(n)				(2,260)

Table 2

OCCUPATIONAL DISTRIBUTION OF BLACK FAMILIES
(in percentages)

Occupational Level	Occupational Sectors			
	Primary Sector	Manufacturing and Mining	Clerical, Sales and Service	Total %
Unskilled laborers	Agricultural laborers	Unskilled non-agricultural laborers	Street vendors, maids, char-workers, etc.	
	3	14	14	31
Semi-skilled laborers		Laborers in mining, trans-portation, ship-ping, etc.	Launderers, cooks, building care employees, etc.	
		24	16	40
Small independent occupations	Farmers & farm managers	Self-employed repairmen, carpenters, etc.	Proprietors of wholesale and retail trade	
	3	1	1	5
Skilled occupations		Skilled workers, craftsmen, me-chanics, repair-men, construc-tion machinery operators	Firemen, police-men, guards, etc.	
		13	3	16
Clerical, sales and low tech-nical occupations			Clerical workers, salesmen, book-keepers, etc.	
			6	6
High technical, professional and managerial occupations			Technicians, man-agers, lawyers, doctors, profes-sors, engineers, etc.	
			2	2
Total %	6	52	42	100
(n)				(261)

Table 3

OCCUPATIONAL DISTRIBUTION OF CASTE-HINDU FAMILIES
(in percentages)

Occupational Level	Occupational Sectors			Total % (n)
	Primary Sector	Manufacturing and Mining	Clerical, Sales and Service	
Unskilled laborers	Agricultural laborers	Unskilled non-agricultural laborers.	Street vendors, messengers, sweepers, etc.	
	9	4	0	13 (181)
Semi-skilled laborers	Semi-skilled agricultural and forestry workers; fishermen	Semi-skilled laborers: construction workers shoemakers, bricklayers	Washermen, domestic and non-domestic servants, barbers, etc.	
	4	2	1	7 (133)
Small independent	Farm tenants	Craftsmen: carpenters, tailors, weavers.	Shopkeepers	
	28	6	7	41 (579)
Skilled occupations and medium level farmers	Small farm owners	Skilled occupations: drivers of motor vehicles, repairers of machines and vehicles.	Firemen, policemen, guards, watchmen, etc.	
	16	2	1	19 (318)
Top level professional and managerial occupations, top level farmers	Big farm owners, landlords.		Clerical occupations, salesmen, teachers, religious personnel, professionals and managers	
	8		12	20 (422)
Total % (n)	65	14	21	100 (1,633)

Table 4

OCCUPATIONAL DISTRIBUTION OF HARIJAN FAMILIES
(in percentages)

	Occupational Sectors			
Occupational Level	*Primary Sector*	*Manufacturing and Mining*	*Clerical, Sales and Service*	*Total % (n)*
Unskilled laborers	Agricultural laborers	Unskilled non-agricultural laborers.	Street vendors, messengers, sweepers, etc.	
	36	16	1	53 (147)
Semi-skilled laborers	Semi-skilled agricultural and forestry workers; fishermen	Semi-skilled laborers: construction workers shoemakers, bricklayers	Washermen, domestic and non-domestic servants, barbers, etc.	
	7	5	1	13 (48)
Small independent	Farm tenants	Craftsmen: carpenters, tailors, weavers.	Shopkeepers	
	14	5	4	23 (88)
Skilled occupations and medium level farmers	Small farm owners	Skilled occupations: drivers of motor vehicles, repairers of machines and vehicles.	Firemen, policemen, guards, watchmen, etc.	
	5	1	2	8 (40)
Top level professional and managerial occupations, top level farmers	Big farm owners, landlords.		Clerical occupations, salesmen, teachers, religious personnel, professionals and managers	
	2		1	3 (8)
Total % (n)	64	27	9	100 (331)

a somewhat higher proportion of whites is found in agriculture as compared to Blacks—ten percent of whites and six percent of Blacks.

If we compare the positions of Blacks and Harijans in relation to the dominant groups in terms of the hierarchical position of their occupations—the figures in the righthand marginal column of each subsection of the table—we find, as we would expect, the deprived groups more often in the lower categories, and less often in the upper categories. In the lowest unskilled set of occupations for the United States, we find thirty-one percent of the Blacks and seven percent of the whites. In India, we find fifty-three percent of the Harijans and thirteen percent of the caste-Hindus. But it is interesting that, despite the fact that there are more in the lowest category in India, the ratio between the dominant and the deprived group in terms of the proportions appearing in this low category is roughly the same in each country—about four times as large a proportion of the deprived group is found in the least-skilled category in comparison with the dominant group. If we consider the highest category in occupations, we find the difference between deprived and dominant groups more striking in each country, with the dominant group seven or eight times as likely to have such an occupation as is the deprived group. The occupations found in that highest category are not themselves directly comparable across nations. In India, we have one fewer category at the top level, and some occupations categorized in the highest category in India (clerical occupations) are categorized lower in the United States. But the comparison within each nation is clear. There is severe occupational deprivation in each country; and a deprivation—at least in terms of level—of roughly similar magnitude.

If we look at the individual cells of Table 1 we find the Harijans heavily concentrated in the category of agricultural laborers— thirty-six percent of them are engaged in such activities. (In general, within the agricultural sector, Harijans are most likely to be landless laborers, while caste-Hindus are more likely to have small independent holdings.) Blacks, on the other hand, tend to concentrate in the unskilled and semi-skilled occupations in manufacturing and service occupations. In both cases, the deprived groups are rarely found in the lower righthand side of the table, where we find white-collar occupations.

Data summarized in Tables 5 and 6 make the relatively low occupational positions of the two depressed groups clearer. The tables present data on the over- and underrepresentation of Blacks and Harijans in various occupations. The figures are simply the difference between the proportions of the entire population and the proportion of the deprived group in each category. A positive figure shows overrepresentation of deprived groups; a negative figure, the opposite.* Within each of the three sectors, Blacks are overrepresented in the lowest-level occupations: laborers and domestic servants. Whites are overrepresented in high-level white-collar occupations. Similarly, Harijans are overrepresented in the lowest-level occupations within each sector as compared with caste-Hindus, who are overrepresented in high-level occupations within each sector. More caste-Hindus are small or big landowners, or clerical workers, or professionals, while the majority of the Harijans are unskilled agricultural laborers or workers.

Education

Education raises the same problem of the differences in the basic population distribution. About ninety-nine percent of the adult Americans have some education, as against only thirty-six percent among Indians. Even if we compare those with some education, we find that only eleven percent of the Indians have secondary and higher education as compared to fifty-three percent of Americans (see table 7).

Consequently, more Blacks are educated than Harijans, and most Blacks are at least literate. Eighty-seven percent of the Harijans report no education, compared to only one percent of Blacks with no education. When Harijans receive some education, it stops at the primary level in most cases. Among our sample, only two percent of Harijans had some high school education and none had any college education, while twenty-two percent of

*Thus the figure of +28% in the upper-left cell (agricultural labor) for India reflects the fact that 36% of Harijans are in that category in comparison with 8% of Indians in general; an "overrepresentation" of Harijans by 28%.

Table 5

OVER- AND UNDERREPRESENTATION OF BLACKS* IN OCCUPATIONS
(Blacks minus entire sample; in percentages)

Occupational Level	Occupational Sectors		
	Primary Sector	Manufacturing and Mining	Clerical, Sales and Service
Unskilled laborers	Agricultural laborers	Unskilled non-agricultural laborers	Street vendors, maids, char-workers, etc.
	+1	+9	+11
Semi-skilled laborers		Laborers in mining, trans-portation, ship-ping, etc.	Launderers, cooks, building care employees, etc.
		+4	+11
Small independent occupations	Farmers & farm managers	Self-employed repairmen, carpenters, etc.	Proprietors of wholesale and retail trade
	−4	−2	−3
Skilled occupations		Skilled workers, craftsmen, me-chanics, repair-men, construc-tion machinery operators	Firemen, police-men, guards, etc.
		−3	+1
Clerical, sales and low techni-cal occupations			Clerical workers, salesmen, book-keepers, etc.
			−12
High technical professional and managerial occupations			Technicians, mana-gers, lawyers, doctors, profes-sors, engineers, etc.
			−13

*+ sign indicates overrepresentation; - sign indicates underrepresentation.

Table 6

OVER- AND UNDERREPRESENTATION OF HARIJANS* IN OCCUPATIONS
(Harijans minus entire Hindu sample; in percentages)

Occupational Level	Occupational Sectors		
	Primary Sector	Manufacturing and Mining	Clerical, Sales and Service
Unskilled laborers	Agricultural laborers	Unskilled non-agricultural laborers	Street vendors, messengers, sweepers, etc.
	+28	+10	+1
Semi-skilled laborers	Semi-skilled agricultural and forestry workers; fishermen	Semi-skilled laborers: construction workers, shoemakers, bricklayers	Washermen, domestic and non-domestic servants, barbers, etc.
	+ 2	+ 2	0
Small independent occupations	Farm tenants	Craftsmen: carpenters, tailors, weavers	Shopkeepers
	−12	0	−2
Skilled occupations and medium level farmers	Small farm owners	Skilled occupations: drivers of motor vehicles, repairers of machines, and vehicles	Firemen, policemen, guards, watchmen, etc.
	− 9	− 1	+1
Top level professional and managerial occupations, top level farmers	Big farm owners, landlords		Clerical occupations, salesmen, teachers, religious personnel, professionals and managers
	− 5		−9

*+ sign indicates overrepresentation; – sign indicates underrepresentation.

Table 7

EDUCATION BY RACE AND CASTE (in percentages)

Education	United States			Education	India		
	United States	White	Black		India	Caste-Hindus	Harijans
None	1	1	1	No education	64	58	87
1-8 years	26	24	39	Some primary	18	21	9
9-11 years	21	20	27	Primary and some middle school	7	9	2
12 years	30	32	22	Middle and some high school	5	5	1
College incomplete	13	13	6	High school completed	3	3	1
College graduate	7	7	4	Some college	2	2	0
College +	3	4	1	Degree and above	1	2	0
Total %	100	100	100	Total %	100	100	100
(n)	(2,521)**	(2,200)	(261)	(n)	(2,126)	(1,776)	(350)
Somers' D*	.26			Somers' D*	.31		

*The statistic used in this and other tables is Somers' D, asymmetric with race or caste as the "independent" variable.

**In this and other tables, the total for the United States is only for the Black and white members of the sample. Twenty-eight cases (one percent of the sample) of "other" races or uncodeable are eliminated.

Blacks had high school education and eleven percent had at least some college education.

If we take high school graduation in the United States and attainment of *any* education in India as measures of minimal educational attainment (a categorization that fits common sense and the distribution of the data, but one that pointedly illustrates the differences between the two societies) we find that in the United States, forty-five percent of our white sample has not finished high school, in comparison with sixty-seven percent of our Black sample. In India, fifty-eight percent of the caste-Hindus report no education, in comparison with eighty-seven percent of the Harijans. At the upper end of the scale, we find eleven percent of our sample of American whites to be college graduates and above, in comparison with five percent of the Black sample. In India, seven percent of the caste-Hindu sample have completed high school or above in comparison with about one percent among Harijans.

The striking contrasts between the two societies makes it difficult for us to answer in any absolutely clear way whether Blacks are relatively less educated than Harijans within the context of their own societies. But we can use a measure of ordinal association—Somers' D—to answer the following questions: If we know that an individual is a Harijan rather than a caste-Hindu, how much more information do we have about his educational level?, And how does this gain in information about education compare with the gain if we know he is Black rather than white? Thus if all Harijans have no education and all caste-Hindus have primary education or better, one would have quite full information on an individual's respective educational attainment if one knew whether he were Harijan or not. In contrast, if there were no difference in the distribution of educational attainments in the two groups, we would have no additional information about educational level by knowing if an individual were a Harijan or a caste-Hindu. In India, Somers' D between caste (dichotomized into Harijan versus caste-Hindus) and education is .31 as compared to a figure of .26 for race and education in the United States. This suggests that we know a bit more about an individual's educational level by knowing whether he is a Harijan or a caste-Hindu than by knowing whether he is Black or White. The comparison does not tell us with certainty that the relative status of Harijan is worse when it comes to education. Part of the information increase depends on the absolute position of Harijans—their concentration in the very lowest category. But it suggests a greater discrepancy in India.

In terms of absolute level of educational attainment and in terms of concentration of the deprived groups in one social category, the situation is clear. Blacks have less education than whites, but almost all have some education and a third have completed high school. Harijans are overwhelmingly concentrated in the category of no education—more than four out of five report that they have no education. Clearly the potential for various kinds of political involvement and activity differs between the two groups.*

---

*We have, in this study, been reporting our own sample data on these basic socioeconomic characteristics. In some cases, more reliable estimates are available from census reports or governmental surveys based on much larger samples. We have chosen to report our sample data, since the items we will report later—political behaviors and political attitudes as well as their relationship to these socioeconomic characteristics—exist only in the sample data.

But a comparison of our data with some other data indicates that estimates based on the sample data are fairly accurate. This is especially encouraging in relation to the data on Blacks and Harijans where our samples are small.

Tables 11 and 12, at the end of this chapter, report data from the Indian census and from the U.S. Bureau of Labor Statistics on educational levels of the four groups with which we are dealing. There is some differences in the categorizations, but the data can be usefully compared with Table 7.

In general, the match is quite good. The major difference seems to be somewhat of an overrepresentation of highly educated Indians (particularly caste-Hindus with higher educational levels) in our sample compared with the census data. However, the census data are about seven years older than our data (and ours also are for only four states), and this may be the source of the difference.

Interestingly enough, the dominant-deprived group disparity (as measured by our measure of association) is quite similar across the two bodies of data in each country. In the United States, Somers' D = .26 is for the sample data and .25 for the data from the Bureau of Labor Statistics. In India, the respective figures for the sample and census data are .31 and .21.

Income

   The comparison of income levels across societies poses some obvious difficulties. Monetary income is not easily translatable from one society to another. And the societies differ in terms of the proportion of income deriving from the monetary sector. We can, however, make some rough comparison (see Table 8).
   Both Blacks and Harijans are more likely to belong to the low-income groups in their respective societies. However, most Harijans are concentrated in the two lowest income levels, while Blacks are more evenly spread over several income levels excepting the highest ones. Thus eighty-one percent of Harijans are in the two lowest income levels as compared to only fifty-three percent of Blacks. The proportion of the Harijans in the three higher-income groups is negligible and there was not a single Harijan family in the income group of Rs. 6,000 and above.
   The comparison of the measures of association suggest that we know a bit more about an individual's income by knowing his race than by knowing his caste.

Socioeconomic Levels

   In Figures 2 and 3 we present a comparison of Blacks and Harijans in terms of their overall socioeconomic levels in their respective societies. This comparison is based on a composite index of socioeconomic status composed of education, income, occupation, and material possessions (see Appendix for the description of how this index was built). The index has been standardized and divided into six equal parts. Such a standardization in a way is artificial, since the two indexes in two different societies are not comparable in any absolute sense. (The lowest sixth in the United States is higher than the lowest sixth in India.) But it enables us to compare the position of Blacks in American society with the position of Harijans in Indian society.
   The data are reported in Figures 2 (for the United States) and 3 (for India). In the lefthand and righthand columns (outside of the graph) we show the proportions of the deprived and dominant groups that are found in each of the six socioeconomic levels. In the graph we show the distribution of each level in terms of the

Table 8

INCOME BY CASTE AND RACE* (in percentages)

Annual Family Income in Dollars	United States			Annual Family Income in Rupees	India		
	United States	White	Black		India	Caste-Hindus	Harijans
Less than 2,000	12	10	26	Under 600	30	26	47
2,000-3,999	17	15	27	601-1,200	30	39	34
4,000-5,999	19	18	21	1,201-2,400	21	23	15
6,000-7,999	18	19	11	2,401-3,600	9	10	3
8,000-9,999	13	14	5	3,601-4,800	4	5	0
10,000-14,999	15	17	6	4,801-6,000	4	5	1
15,000 and above	7	8	4	6,001 and above	3	3	0
Total %	100	100	100	Total %	100	100	100
(n)	(2,358)	(2,111)	(247)	(n)	(2,003)	(1,665)	(338)
Somers' D	.38			Somers' D	.34		

*For those with valid answers.

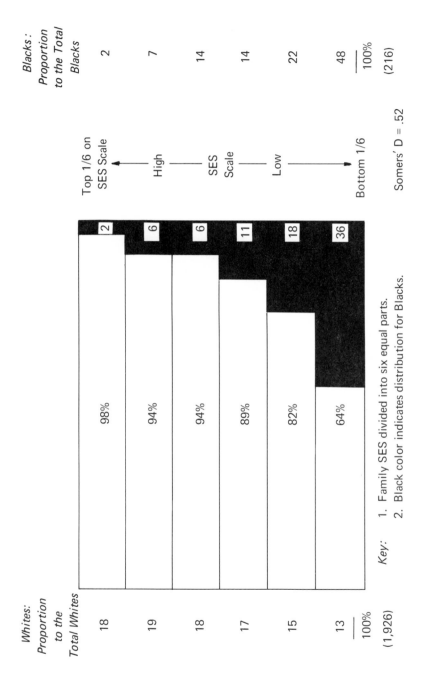

Key: 1. Family SES divided into six equal parts.
         2. Black color indicates distribution for Blacks.

Figure 2

FAMILY SOCIOECONOMIC STATUS (SES) OF WHITES AND BLACKS

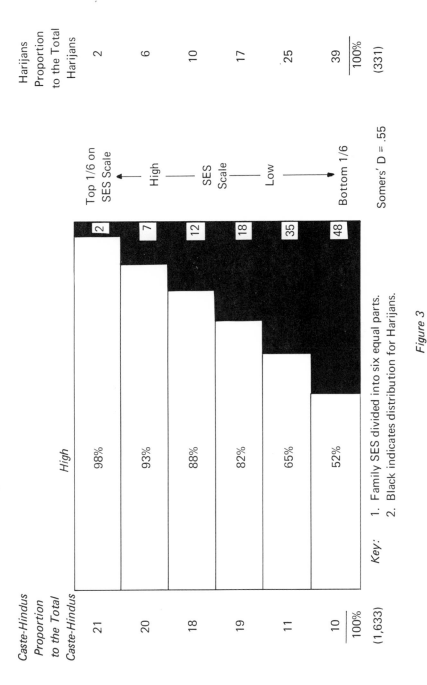

Figure 3

FAMILY SOCIOECONOMIC STATUS (SES) OF CASTE-HINDUS AND HARIJANS

proportion from the deprived and the dominant groups. If the groups had the same dsitribution of socioeconomic types, we would find, on each level, that there would be the same proportion of deprived and dominant group members as their proportion in the population as a whole. As one can see, the situation is quite different.

Blacks are about eleven percent of our sample, but they are thirty-six percent of the lowest socioeconomic level of the American society. As we go up the ladder of socioeconomic level, the representation of the Blacks decreases. Thus only two percent of the highest level—that is the top sixth of the population in receipt of the benefits of society—is Black, instead of the eleven percent we would find if there were equality.

We find the same pattern of socio-economic levels with regard to Harijans and caste-Hindus. Harijans form about sixteen percent of our Hindu sample in India, but they form about half of the lowest sixth of socioeconomic status in India, and only 2 percent of the highest sixth.

But, as compared to Harijans, Blacks are more concentrated in the lowest category of the scale of their society. Consider the distribution of the two groups into the six levels as reported in the far right columns of Figures 2 and 3. Thirty-nine percent of the Harijans are in the lowest sixth, as compared to forty-eight percent among Blacks.

However, in general, the pattern of distribution is remarkably similar. This is reflected in the fact that the measure of association between race and position on the socioeconomic scale is .52 and between caste and position in the scale, it is .55. The magnitude of the association indicates that one has a great deal of information indeed on the social status of an individual by knowing his race or caste.

The data reported thus far on socioeconomic characteristics hold no surprises. The deprived groups are deprived. On some of the individual measures such as education and income, one might infer that the Harijans are relatively more deprived than the Blacks, but that is in part a result of the fact that Harijans are concentrated much more at the very bottom category of the various hierarchies. When one takes a more standardized measure—as we do in Figures 2 and 3—we find a roughly similar pattern of deprivation vis-à-vis the dominant group. Relative to the dominant groups, Blacks and Harijans are in a similar position in each society.

The absolute difference, however, is quite striking between the two deprived groups across the nations. Harijans are absolutely much worse off than Blacks. And they are the more concentrated in the lowest categories of the hierarchies. Blacks have lower education than whites, but they have a wide spread of education levels; on the other hand, Harijans are overwhelmingly uneducated. Blacks have low status occupations, but there are some with higher status clerical and professional occupations. Harijans almost never appear in these categories.

The data do suggest that, in comparison with Blacks, Harijans will have a difficult time developing internal leadership on the basis of which organized group activity can begin; and, in addition, the limitations of the education attainment of Harijans make the task of that leadership more difficult, since the problem of communication to the mass-base would be greater. This fact is underlined if we consider two other characteristics—exposure to the mass media, and knowledge of some other language.

Table 9 compares the four groups in terms of their exposure to the mass media: listening to the radio (watching TV in the United States), reading newspapers, and reading magazines. There is a small Black-white difference in exposure, a difference that is greater in terms of exposure to more than one medium—indicating that Blacks are more likely to be limited to television as the medium of exposure. Similarly, fewer Harijans read newspapers, listen to the radio, or go to movies than do caste-Hindus. Comparing across the nations, we find fewer Harijans than Blacks exposed to the mass media. Indeed, almost all Blacks have some exposure, while half the Harijans have none. The discrepancy between the Harijans and caste-Hindus in terms of exposure to mass media of communication is greater than between Blacks and whites (Somers' D's of .33 and .16 respectively).

An additional relevant bit of information is presented in Table 10. The organizational potential of Blacks and Harijans differed, we argued, because of the dispersion of Harijans into different linguistic groups—a dispersion that makes communication difficult across the groups. In Table 10 we report some data on language

Table 9

EXPOSURE TO MASS MEDIA OF COMMUNICATION BY CASTE AND RACE (in percentages)

	United States			India		
	United States	White	Black	India	Caste-Hindus	Harijans
No exposure	4	4	7	31	27	50
Only watch TV or read newspaper or magazines / Only listen to radio, read newspaper or go to movies	25	23	36	24	23	27
Two of the above three	48	50	38	19	20	13
All three	23	24	19	26	30	11
Total %	100	100	100	100	100	100
(n)	(3,059)	(2,653)	(406)	(2,130)	(1,779)	(351)
Somers' D	.16			.33		

Table 10

KNOWLEDGE OF ADDITIONAL LANGUAGE BY CASTE

(in percentages)

Language	India	Caste-Hindus	Harijans
No other language	87	85	95
Additional Indian language	10	11	4
English	3	4	1
Total %	100	100	100
(n)	(2,130)	(1,779)	(351)

knowledge for caste-Hindus and Harijans. In general, few caste-Hindus or Harijans know a second language, but the situation is more severe among Harijans. Only four percent report knowing a second language, and less than one percent knows English, an important *lingua franca* for cross-group communication.

In sum, the data support our description of the Blacks and Harijans as deprived groups and our expectation that Harijans would be absolutely more deprived. The absolute level of deprivation may have significant consequences for the amount and type of political activity in which they engage. To that question we now turn.

Appendix to Chapter III

Table 11

EDUCATIONAL LEVELS OF BLACKS AND WHITES*

(1966; in percentages)

Educational Levels	United States**	White	Negro
No schooling	2	2	4
1-8 years	30	29	46
9-12 years	49	50	41
Some college (1-3 years)	9	9	5
4 years or more of college	10	10	4
Total %	100	100	100
(n in thousands)	(103,025)	(93,415)	(9,610)

Somers' D = .25

SOURCE: Bureau of Labor Statistics, *Current Population Reports,* "Negro Population," March, 1968. (Computed)

*Includes only population 25 years old and above.

**Figures for the United States have been computed as sum of white and Black.

Table 12

EDUCATIONAL LEVELS OF HARIJANS AND NON-HARIJANS
(1961; in percentages)

	India	*Non-Harijans*	*Harijans*
Illiterate	76	74	90
Literate (without educational level)	15	15	7
Primary or junior basic	7	9	3
High school and above	2	2	*
Total %	100	100	100
(n in millions)	(488.9)	(424.5)	(64.4)
Somers' D = .21			

SOURCE: The Census of India Reports, 1961 (Computed)

*Less than half percent

Chapter IV

THE POLITICAL ORIENTATIONS
OF BLACKS AND HARIJANS

Our major concern is with political behavior, but let us begin with a consideration of the degree and type of subjective involvement in political life of the groups we are comparing. The extent to which these groups are subjectively involved in politics and the ways in which they are involved should tell us much about their relationship to the political system. Furthermore, knowledge of the subjective orientations of the various groups should help us understand the "meaning" of their participation to them; that is, what are the attitudes and beliefs that accompany the political activity of various groups? And, lastly, these attitudes are part of the causal paths that lead to participation; paths we shall later explore.

We shall consider four types of political orientation:

(1) general involvement in politics: interest in and concern about political matters and information about politics;

(2) partisan attachment;

(3) perception of the government as a relevant institution for dealing with the problems facing the individual; and

(4) group consciousness: awareness of the particular political relevance of one's own group.

These four sets of political orientations all relate to the general politicization of a population—whereby individuals become in some way subjectively involved in political matters. But they represent somewhat different types of orientation and imply different types of involvement.

(1) *General interest in politics* implies a civic concern with the issues facing one's community or nation; coupled with *information* it would identify for us those who are generally politically involved.

(2) *Partisan attachment* represents an alternative mode of subjective involvement in the political process—through attachment to a political party. Such attachment may mean many things: It may represent the passionate commitment of a true believer to a revolutionary party; it may represent habitual transfer of attachment from generation to generation; it may reflect exposure to political leaders eager to gain support. In our case, the nature of the parties involved generally rules out the first interpretation. And what we know of party affiliation from studies in the United States and from some analysis of our Indian data suggests that the·last two types of interpretation are more meaningful. Partisan attachment grows from exposure to the party either across generations or in one's lifetime and represents a more passive and less "self-generated" involvement than does interest or information.

(3) *Perception of the government as relevant to one's own needs* reflects a particularly personal and important type of political involvement, whereby individuals—whatever their

general view of political life—see the government as the relevant institution for dealing with their problems. And, lastly

(4) *group consciousness* is a form of political involvement particularly important for our understanding of the political behavior of deprived groups. Are they self-consciously aware of the role of the deprived group to which they belong as actors in the political system?

General Interest in Politics

Let us begin by considering the extent to which the two deprived groups are interested in politics. Table 13 compares Blacks and whites and Harijans and caste-Hindus in terms of their interest in politics. The measure here is a composite of a number of questions—how interested respondents were in national politics, and how much they discussed national politics and affairs and local political affairs. In each country, the deprived group is less interested in politics than is the dominant group, with the difference somewhat greater between Harijans and caste-Hindus. The data as presented in Table 13 do not easily allow direct comparison across the countries. It would be hard, with questions as general as these, to agree what comparable levels of political involvement might be. Furthermore, the cutting points on the scales are different—though this may actually help us to make some direct comparisons. In the United States, almost all respondents, Black or white, express some interest in politics and engage in at least some discussion of local or national politics. Therefore the lowest category on the scale contains individuals who express some political interest. In India, those in the category designated "low" are in a category that could be designated "none"—they report no political interest or discussion. If we use this more stringent criterion of having no interest to compare Blacks and Harijans, we find that almost half of the Harijans report no involvement in politics, but almost none (less than two percent) of the Blacks so report. This sharp gap between Blacks and Harijans does not reflect the difference in their relative positions in the two societies—though Blacks are more like the

Table 13

INTEREST IN POLITICS BY RACE AND CASTE (in percentages)

Level of Interest	United States			India		
	Total	White	Black	Total	Caste-Hindus	Harijans
Low	24	22	31	35	35	47
Medium	44	45	41	33	32	34
High	32	33	28	32	34	20
Total %	100	100	100	100	100	100
(n)	(2,521)	(2,260)	(261)	(2,130)	(1,779)	(351)
Somers' D		.09			.18	

dominant group than are Harijans—but reflects the absolute levels of interest in the two societies.

Information

The data on information will be of special interest later in this work because they help us interpret the nature of different political acts. We present the simple comparison among the four groups in terms of amount of information here because the data are of interest, but we do so with some unease lest the reader be unaware of some ambiguities in the meaning of the comparisons. The data on information are in one way easier to interpret than are the data on interest. In another way, they are harder to interpret. The information questions are much more reliable indicators than are the interest questions; in relation to interest, respondents may adjust their answers to what they think of as the proper answer (and over- or understate their interest in politics). And the phenomenon of interest is itself so ambiguous that the answers may be somewhat unreliable—how one describes one's interest today may differ from the description tomorrow. The information questions, on the other hand, require factual knowledge of names of people or the working of the government to obtain a correct answer; we are more likely to obtain an accurate measure of "real" information than of "real" interest.

The greater ambiguity of the meaning of the information questions lies in the choice of questions: what are equivalent items of information in the two countries such that one can compare scores across the countries? Is knowledge of the name of the MP equivalent to knowledge of the name of a Congressman, or a Senator, or what? The actual questions used are listed in the Appendix. They are mostly questions in which respondents had to identify particular individuals, though there are some others as well. The reader should keep in mind that "highly informed" means the ability to answer many of these questions. In some sense, the ambiguity as to whether we are measuring equivalent levels of information if we obtain equivalent scores across the countries, is as ambiguous when we compare the deprived and the dominant groups in each of the countries. The questions we ask are generally about the dominant groups—that is, the leaders that respondents are asked to identify are rarely Black (except for an occasional local official or member of Congress) and rarely Harijan (with similar occasional exceptions). What level of information we would have found if we had asked questions more directly relevant to the deprived groups is not certain.

This introduction to the information questions is not to suggest that they should be dismissed. They do contain useful indications of how much the various groups know of the political life of their communities and nations—and if this is skewed in the direction of information about the dominant segments of the community and nation, this merely reflects political reality—and the information variables will be useful later in trying to differentiate among types of political activities. But one ought to be cautious about inferences drawn from the distribution of answers.

The data on information are presented in Table 14. In the United States only about one percent of the sample (of whites or Blacks) could answer none of our questions correctly, in comparison with about half the Indian sample. We, therefore, report the data for Americans who could answer two or fewer questions and for Indians who could answer none. The data reveal that the difference between the dominant and deprived groups is of about the same magnitude in each of the countries (if we take Somers' D—a measure of ordinal relationships—as a measure of this), with the deprived groups substantially less well informed— the interpretation of those figures, of course, subject to all the qualifications made earlier. And the difference between the deprived and dominant groups seems to be greater on information measures than on interest measures, as reported in Table 13. The measure of association in the United States is .09 between race and interest and .24 between race and information; and, in India, the caste-interest relationship is .18 while the caste-information association is .26.

Partisan Attachment

Let us turn to another subjective measure of political involvement: partisanship. Political parties may be important for many reasons: they may be major instrumentalities for relating citizens to their government, for mobilizing citizens, for organizing

Table 14

LEVELS OF INFORMATION ON POLITICAL MATTERS, BY RACE AND CASTE (in percentages)

Number of Correct Answers	United States			Number of Correct Answers	India		
	Total	White	Black		Total	Caste-Hindus	Harijans
2 questions or less correct...	18	16	33	None correct...	51	47	69
3 to 6 questions correct...	54	54	52	1 to 3 correct...	28	29	24
More than 6 questions correct...	28	30	15	4 or more correct...	21	25	6
Total %	100	100	100	Total %	100	100	100
(n)...	(2,521)	(2,260)	(261)	(n)...	(2,130)	(1,779)	(351)
Somers' D	.24				.26		

social choice through electoral mechanisms; and parties are, according to some theorists, the major way in which the mass participation of a citizenry is institutionalized. The last point is important. It implies that participation, if structured by parties, is a more controlled, meaningful, and institutionalized mode of participation. Participation of unaffiliated citizens is more "anomic," less effective, but more likely to create serious social tensions. Much data—particularly in the United States—have shown that party affiliation is a major anchor point for political attitudes; it structures the political world in ways that would not be otherwise possible. But note one distinction: from the point of view of the political system, party affiliation represents a way in which participation is institutionalized; from the point of view of the individual citizen, it may represent a way in which he is mobilized by others into politics. In other words, the degree to which partisanship is widespread may represent the extent to which parties are active but, under certain circumstances, the extent to which individual partisans are passive.

In any case, the data on partisanship reported in Table 15 are quite striking, particularly in comparison with the data on interest and information. Previous tables showed the more deprived groups to be substantially less politically interested and less politically informed; but the data on partisanship show little difference between the deprived and dominant groups. In India, Harijans are almost as likely to be strong partisan supporters as are caste-Hindus. They are somewhat more likely, on the other hand, to be categorized as "no party." (This ought not to be interpreted as principled independence from political parties; it is more likely to involve passive lack of awareness of parties.) What is interesting is the fact that Harijans, when they are partisan, are more likely to be strong partisans than are caste-Hindus. If we take out from Table 7 forty-four percent of Harijans who did not support any party and take the remaining fifty-six percent Harijans who are partisans and then compute the percentages of those who are strong partisans from among those who are partisans then we find that seventy-five percent of the fifty-six percent Harijans who are partisans are strong partisans. But if we compute the percentages of strong partisans from among the sixty-eight percent partisan caste-Hindus (after taking out thirty-two percent of the

Table 15

PARTISANSHIP BY RACE AND CASTE (in percentages)

| Partisanship* | United States | | | India | | |
	Total	White	Black	Total	Caste- Hindus	Harijans
No party	8	8	4	35	32	44
Weak partisans	14	14	12	9	10	5
Moderate partisans	44	45	35	13	14	10
Strong partisans	35	33	50	43	44	41
Total %	100	100	100	100	100	100
(n)	(2,521)	(2,260)	(261)	(2,130)	(1,779)	(351)
Somers' D	−.19**			.08		

*Strong partisans are those who report they support a party and that they are strong supporters. Moderate partisans are those who say they support a party, but do not consider themselves strong partisans. Weak partisans are those who say they do not support a party, but when asked if there is any party they prefer over the others, mention a party. "No party" include those who say they are "independent" but also those who answer the above question negatively.

**A negative value for Somers' D means that the deprived group has a "higher" value on the variable being measured.

caste-Hindus who do not support any party) than we find that
sixty-five percent of the partisan caste-Hindus are strong partisans.
In other words, Harijans are more likely than caste-Hindus to have
no party affiliation, but if they express affiliation they are more
likely to express a strong affiliation.

In the United States, Blacks are more likely to be partisans and,
if partisan, to be strong partisans. One-half of the American Blacks
describe themselves as strong partisans, compared with one-third
of the whites.

The data are particularly striking in India in light of the
following considerations: In the first place, the question that
produced the data is a difficult one. In order for an individual to
be coded as a partisan—strong, moderate, or weak—he had to
mention the name of the party with which he is affiliated. He was
not given cues—that is, he was not asked, "Do you support the
Congress party?" but, "Which party do you support?" and so on.
Whereas only thirty-three percent of the Harijan sample could
answer one or more of the information questions correctly,
fifty-six percent named a party—in most cases, of course, the
Congress—with which they felt some sense of affiliation. And the
phenomenon is paralleled by the data on caste-Hindus. More name
a party with which they are affiliated (sixty-eight percent) than
could answer any of our political questions correctly (fifty-three
percent). This does not necessarily mean that party affiliation
exists among totally uninformed people. The information
questions may, indeed, be more difficult than the identification of
some political party, and if we had asked easier information
questions we would have found many people more able to answer
them. But as can be seen from the list in the Appendix, the
information items are fairly simple. Thus, it does seem a
remarkably high level of partisan self-identification for a
population that is otherwise not terribly politically sophisticated.

In the United States, the pattern is parallel—with Blacks much
more partisan than one might expect from their interest and
information differences with whites. However, the data are not
quite that striking in that the Black population is absolutely more
informed than the Harijans.

These data do not necessarily indicate that parties are well
institutionalized in the two countries. At least, they tell us nothing

about the parties as decision-making units, as organizers of political choice, and so forth. What they do tell us is that in India and in the United States, the parties—to be more precise the Congress Party and the Democratic party—are the foci for the subjective identification of deprived groups. And, particularly in India, they have penetrated the consciousness of many otherwise apolitical people. The data suggest that the role of partisanship as a means of mobilizing individuals to politics will deserve careful consideration.

The Relevance of Government

The data thus far do not indicate that the two deprived groups we are comparing are particularly politically aroused; they are as likely or more likely to have affiliations with a political party, but they are somewhat less interested in politics and quite a bit less informed. But one must be careful in interpreting the data as indicating that these groups are not conscious of political and governmental matters. Information and interest do tend to refer to the dominant political life of the respective societies. Where these matters impinge more closely on the lives of the deprived groups, they may be quite aware. One area in which there is more political awareness among Blacks than among whites, and as much awareness among Harijans as among caste-Hindus, has to do with the perception of the government as a relevant institution for dealing with the respondent's own problems. In our questionnaire we asked respondents about their most pressing personal and family problems. In relation to these most salient problems—self-defined by the respondents—we then asked what persons or institutions they considered most relevant for solving these problems, or did they have to solve the problems themselves? Table 16 compares the four groups in terms of the proportions which mentioned the government as the relevant problem-solving agency. In the United States, the difference is quite sharp, with Blacks much more likely to mention the government as the relevant agency for problem-solving (thirty-nine percent in comparison with twenty-three percent among whites). In India, the pattern is different. Caste-Hindus and Harijans are as likely to mention the government as the potential agency for problem-

Table 16

MENTIONING OF GOVERNMENT AS SOURCE OF HELP
FOR SOLVING PERSONAL PROBLEMS (among those
mentioning personal problems), BY RACE AND CASTE
(in percentages)

Government as Solver of Personal Problems	United States			India		
	Total	White	Black	Total	Caste-Hindus	Harijans
Mention government	25	23	39	37	37	37
Do not mention government	75	77	61	63	63	63
Total %	100	100	100	100	100	100
(n)	(1,773)	(1,572)	(201)	(2,130)	(1,779)	(351)

solving. Thirty-seven percent of each group does. These results are interesting for two reasons: For one thing, they suggest a generally higher degree of governmental expectation among Indians than among Americans. The Indian sample as a whole mentions the government about as frequently as do Black Americans and much more frequently than do white Americans. Direct comparisons across the two nations on questions of this sort must be interpreted with caution, for proportions answering one way or another can so easily be affected by question-wording and the like. But in this instance, the nature of the questions makes the difference particularly worth noting. The problem for which respondents mention the government as relevant is the most pressing personal or family problem as defined by the respondent. In this sense, governmental expectations are linked into the respondent's own schedule of priorities and, we assume, have meaning for him. Secondly, the question that elicited or did not elicit a response that the government was the institution that "could help solve the problem" was an open-ended question. The respondent had to volunteer the governmental reference. Thus, the higher frequency of such mentions in India may reflect a higher level of politicization.

The second interesting fact about the Indian data is the similarity between Harijans and caste-Hindus. When it came to information and general involvement in politics, Harijans were quite a bit less politicized than were caste-Hindus. But when it comes to the perception of the government as relevant vis-à-vis the self-defined personal problems of the respondent, they are as politicized.

Clearly, this indicates that any blanket notion of politicization—as an awareness and involvement in politics—is not valid. Harijans and (to a lesser extent) Blacks may be less politically aware and involved when it comes to the general world of politics outside of their own realm of concern, but when it comes to politics and government as they impinge on Blacks' and Harijans' self-defined life space, this is no longer the case.

Group Consciousness

One other bit of data confirms the picture of the Blacks and, to a lesser extent, the Harijans as politically conscious in relation to problems that impinge more closely on their own lives—in particular, in relation to their own problems and those of their own group. Respondents were asked to describe conflicts in their communities. In India and in the United States, they were asked to describe the conflicting groups. In the United States, they were also asked to describe the subject of the conflict. In some sense, one can think of this question as attempting to use respondents as informants; not to tell us their opinions or about their behavior, but about events in their communities. But, of course, individuals perceive their communities from their own perspectives. Our assumption had been that a deprived group would be more aware of controversy between itself and the dominant group than would the dominant group. In the United States, the data are clear on this. When asked about the groups that are in conflict within the community, seventeen percent of the Blacks report that there is conflict between the races in comparison with nine percent of the whites, and twenty-five percent report that the subject of the dispute is race, in comparison with eleven percent of the whites (Table 17).

The Indian data are parallel, with some differences. Harijans are somewhat more likely to report conflict among castes than are caste-Hindus, but the difference is less and the general level of reporting of such conflicts is lower.*

---

*This ought not to be taken as an absolute measure of the amount of caste conflict in Indian villages. Caste conflict may be at the basis of conflicts described by respondents in other terms—between landowners and tenants, and so forth.

The same pattern of heightened group consciousness among Blacks is found in answers to several other questions in our survey on the major problems facing the individual, the community, and the nation. Blacks are much more likely than whites to mention problems having to do with race. (Sixty-three percent of Blacks mention such problems in comparison with thirty-nine percent of whites). These particular questions cannot be used for tapping group consciousness in India, since the economic and subsistence problems were so frequently mentioned as the major problem in India that few references are found to group affiliations as the basis of a personal, community, or national problem.

For later analyses we shall use the more inclusive measure of group consciousness among Blacks, whereby they may refer to race problems or to

SUMMATION

In sum, we find some general similarity in the subjective orientations to politics between Blacks and Harijans, or rather, similarity in their relative positions vis-à-vis the dominant groups in their society. In both cases, the deprived groups are less informed about politics at large and are somewhat less interested. On the other hand, in both cases, their "deprivation" vis-à-vis the dominant group does not extent to partisanship. Harijans are about as likely to be partisans as are caste-Hindus, and Blacks more likely than whites. And when it comes to the belief that governmental action is relevant to the solution of their own problems and to their consciousness of group as measured by perception of conflict between themselves and the dominant group, they are more "politicized" than the dominant group.

There are, however, important differences between the two deprived groups. When it comes to those dimensions on which the deprived groups are "lower" than the dominant groups—in particular to information and interest in politics—Harijans are relatively "worse off" than Blacks; that is, they differ from the dominant group more. And in absolute terms they are clearly less informed or interested than Blacks. These comparisons are tricky at best, but the magnitude of the difference is substantial enough to make it clear that the differences are real. Conversely, when it comes to those dimensions where the deprived group indicates as much or more political consciousness as the dominant group—as with partisanship, or belief in the relevance of the government to one's own problems, or the self-consciousness of one's group—Blacks are relatively more conscious than Harijans. Thus Harijans are about as partisan as caste-Hindus, but Blacks are more partisan than whites; Harijans are a touch more likely to see the government as relevant to their own problems than are

---

racial conflict in order to be categorized as "group conscious." And for distinguishing "group conscious" Harijans from other Harijans we shall use a more inclusive measure based on caste references in answers to open questions on community conflict as well as on the most influential groups in the community.

Table 17

GROUP CONSCIOUSNESS: PROPORTION SEEING COMMUNITY CONFLICT
AS INVOLVING RACE OR CASTE CONFLICT (in percentages)

United States	Total	White	Black
Percentage mentioning races as the subject of community conflict	13	11	25
Percentage mentioning races as the participants in community conflict	10	9	17
(n)	(2,521)	(2,260)	(261)

India	Total	Caste-Hindus	Harijans
Percentage mentioning castes as the participants in community conflict	5	5	7
(n)	(2,130)	(1,779)	(351)

caste-Hindus; Blacks are substantially more so than whites; and the same pattern holds for conflict awareness. One can summarize the difference between the deprived and dominant groups across the nations, perhaps as reflecting similarities of patterns at different levels of development; that is, at different levels of political consciousness.

Let us return to this question when we have looked at some data on political behavior.

Chapter V

POLITICAL ACTIVITIES

As pointed out above, we have been dealing with four modes of
political activity—voting, campaign activity, cooperative activity,
and citizen-initiated contacts. The data comparing our four groups
on these modes of participation are contained in Tables 18
through 21. The tables contain three types of information. We
present the frequencies for political activity of the four groups;
the measure of association (Somers' D) between race or caste and
the mode of participation; and a "representation ratio" for Blacks
and Harijans. The latter is an index of the over- or
underrepresentation of the deprived group in the activist
population. Thus if Blacks are as likely to be in the population of
regular voters as they are in the population as a whole, they would
have a representation ratio of 1.0. If they are half as frequently

Table 18

FREQUENCY OF VOTING BY RACE AND CASTE

(in percentages)

Voting Frequency	United States			India		
	Total	White	Black	Total	Caste-Hindus	Harijans
Never vote	18	16	26	17	18	14
Vote occasionally	36	36	37	39	38	41
Vote regularly	46	48	38	44	44	45
Total %	100	100	100	100	100	100
(n)	(2,521)	(2,260)	(261)	(2,126)	(1,776)	(350)
Representation ratio in voting population	Blacks .82			Harijans 1.0		
Somers' D	.13			−.03		

among the regular voters as their proportion in the overall population, they have a ratio of .5. Or if they are twice as frequently found, they would have a ratio of 2.0. This is a simple and useful measure of the extent to which a group is "deprived" or "advantaged" in relation to some political act.

The result can be briefly summarized, since the patterns are fairly clear. When it comes to voting (Table 18), Harijans are not "deprived" at all; their ratio of representation is 1, indicating that they are as likely to vote as are caste-Hindus. In comparison, Blacks vote somewhat less frequently than whites with a representation ratio of .82.* When it comes to campaign participation (Table 19), both deprived groups are less active than the dominant groups. It is somewhat ambiguous where the difference between the deprived and dominant group is greater. The Harijans have a lower representation ratio than Blacks (.65 in comparison with .80) but Somers' D is greater for the association between race and campaign activity. The divergence derives from the fact that the representation ratio is based only on the most active category, while the measure of association refers to the entire distribution. The divergence, therefore, reflects a somewhat sharper difference between Harijans and caste-Hindus in the most active category of the scale, while they are more similar at the low end of the scale. This suggests that Harijans, if they get involved in campaign activity, are less likely to become very active.

When it comes to cooperative participation (Table 20), there is divergence. Blacks do not differ from whites in the frequency with which they engage in such activities, but Harijans differ from caste-Hindus. There are fewer Indians than Americans active in this way, but among the few who are active, Harijans are clearly underrepresented. What cooperative activity there is in India is more likely to be carried on by the dominant group than by the deprived group.

Lastly we come to citizen-initiated contacts (Table 21), where we find quite a bit of similarity between the countries. In both

---

*Table 26, at the end of this chapter, reports from an extensive U.S. Bureau of the Census survey of voting rates for Blacks and whites. Since it deals with voting in a particular election, it is not directly comparable to our data, but the magnitude of the Black-white difference is roughly the same as in our sample data.

Table 19

PARTICIPATION IN PARTY AND CAMPAIGN ACTIVITIES
BY RACE AND CASTE (in percentages)

Level of Activity	United States			India		
	Total	White	Black	Total	Caste-Hindus	Harijans
Inactive	46	45	54	67	66	70
Somewhat inactive	29	29	27	23	22	24
Very active	25	26	20	10	11	7
Total %	100	100	100	100	100	100
(n)	(2,521)	(2,260)	(261)	(2,126)	(1,776)	(350)
Representation ratio in campaign activities	Blacks .80			Harijans .65		
Somers' D	.10			.04		

Table 20

PARTICIPATION IN COOPERATIVE ACTIVITY
BY RACE AND CASTE (in percentages)

Participation in Cooperative Activity	United States			India		
	Total	White	Black	Total	Caste-Hindus	Harijans
Inactive	53	53	54	78	77	82
Somewhat active	25	25	26	15	16	14
Very active	22	22	21	7	8	4
Total	100	100	100	100	100	100
(n)	(2,521)	(2,260)	(261)	(2,126)	(1,776)	(350)
Representation ratio	Blacks .93			Harijans .56		
Somers' D	.01			.05		

cases, the deprived groups are less active in this way. The representation ratios are such as to suggest that they are in each case about half as likely to engage in such activity as one would expect from their proportion of the population.

The pattern of results is most interesting. Harijans have been most incorporated into the political process in relationship to voting; here they are as active as the dominant group. In comparison, Blacks are somewhat less active in voting, a situation that probably reflects different historical developments of the electoral systems in the two countries. The United States has a long tradition of discrimination in voting and this is probably reflected in the voting differences; an interpretation supported by the fact that the association (Somers' D), between race and voting in the South is .16 and only .02 in the North. In India, the electoral system expanded suddenly and fully to encompass all Indians and has been the symbol of the aspirations for a universalistic and equalitarian citizenship.

In relation to campaign activity, the relationship between the two pairs of groups is similar. But in relation to the other two types of activity—cooperative activity and citizen-initiated contacts—the pattern is most interesting.

Let us consider citizen-initiated contacts more closely. We are dealing here with acts that have rarely been studied by those interested in political participation. These are the contacts that individuals make with some governmental official in relation to some problem that the individuals consider important. Each of these acts may be relatively unimportant from the point of view of the overall activity of political institutions. But for the individual—particularly the deprived individual—such acts may be of great importance. For one thing, it is only in relation to contacts initiated by the individual that he can "set the agenda" of the political interaction—that is, he can choose the subject matter of the contact. And this means that he can direct the contact to those narrow, particularized problems that may be of greatest importance to him. Furthermore, though any single act may have little impact on the overall distribution of benefits in the society, the sum of all these acts may have a major impact. Thus the degree of deprivation in what one might call the "politics of everyday life" is particularly interesting.

Table 21

CITIZEN-INITIATED CONTACT WITH GOVERNMENT
OFFICIALS AND POLITICAL LEADERS,
BY RACE AND CASTE (in percentages)

| Contact | United States | | | India | | |
	Total	White	Black	Total	Caste-Hindus	Harijans
Not contacted any elite	69	67	85	81	79	89
Contacted	31	33	15	19	21	11
Total %	100	100	100	100	100	100
(n)	(2,521)	(2,260)	(261)	(2,126)	(1,776)	(350)
Representation ratio	Blacks .48			Harijans .59		
Somers' D	.19			.10		

Blacks and Harijans are similar in that they are quite deprived vis-à-vis contacts; a fact consistent with our expectation that the ascriptive characteristic of these groups would create particular boundaries over which they would have difficulty crossing, and one of the boundaries is between the deprived groups and officialdom, most of whose members are of the dominant group. The nature of these boundaries is suggested in Tables 22, 24 and 25. Table 22 reports answers to a question on whether or not the respondent thought that a go-between would be needed if he wanted to approach a government official. Blacks are more than twice as likely as whites to think that a go-between would be needed; half of the former and about one-fifth of the latter think this. In India, many more respondents in general thought a go-between necessary, but the dominant-deprived groups relationship is similar to that in the United States, though the difference is less sharp. Harijans more frequently report a go-between necessary. Table 23 adds one more bit of information to our understanding of Blacks and Harijans as contactors (or, rather, as noncontactors). Respondents were asked whether they believed they could find a go-between if they needed one. In both cases, those in the deprived group are less likely to report that they believe they could find such a go-between than are the members of the dominant group. And on this measure, the difference between Harijans and caste-Hindus is greater than that between Blacks and whites.

The situation is summed up in Table 24, where we report the proportion of the various groups who have:

(1) actually contacted the government;

(2) have not contacted the government but report that they could contact directly if they wanted to;

(3) have not contacted, think one needs a go-between, and believe they could find one; and lastly

(4) the proportion who believes one needs a go-between but believes also that they would have trouble finding one.

The difference between Blacks and whites is quite striking. A third of the Blacks are in the last category, in contrast with thirteen percent of the whites. At the other end of the table, we find a full

Table 22

PERCEIVED ABILITY TO CONTACT GOVERNMENTAL
AND POLITICAL ELITE DIRECTLY BY RACE AND CASTE

(in percentages)

Contact	United States			India		
	Total	*White*	*Black*	*Total*	*Caste-Hindus*	*Harijans*
Connections necessary to contact the elite	25	21	52	49	46	60
Depends	3	3	3	5	6	2
Can contact the elite directly	72	76	45	46	49	38
Total %	100	100	100	100	100	100
(n)	(2,351)	(2,114)	(237)	(2,126)	(1,776)	(350)
Somers' D		.32			.20	

Table 23

EASY AVAILABILITY OF CONNECTIONS FOR
CONTACTING ELITE (for those who need connections
to approach the elite; in percentages)

Contact	United States			India		
	Total	White	Black	Total	Caste- Hindus	Harijans
Cannot find connections	5	5	7	6	5	11
May find connections	37	35	43	44	41	51
Can easily find connections	58	61	50	50	54	38
Total %	100	100	100	100	100	100
(n)	(497)	(379)	(118)	(1,063)	(817)	(187)

seventy-nine percent of the whites have either contacted or believe they could, if they wanted to, contact officials directly. But only forty-eight percent of the Blacks are in these categories. In India, the pattern is quite similar, though the distinction is not quite as sharp between the deprived and the dominant groups.

The data do add up to a picture of frustration for the deprived groups in contrast with the dominant group, and a frustration that might be more severe among Blacks than among Harijans. This is summarized in Figure 4. There we compare the proportions of the four groups which sees the government as relevant to their problems with those who are active in contacting the government.

We can assume that the deprived groups have more serious personal and family problems than do the dominant groups; an assumption consistent with the data we have presented on objective social status and consistent with data we have as to their subjectively perceived personal and family problems. For instance, when asked to name the major personal or family problems they face, seventy-one percent of the Harijans mention problems that could be considered subsistence problems—adequate food and clothing—in comparison with fifty-two percent of the caste-Hindus. In the United States, the comparable figures are nineteen percent for Blacks and six percent for whites. These figures are based on additional data analysis not reported here in a table. The absolute level of subsistence needs is, of course, higher in India, but the relationship between the dominant and deprived groups is the same.

What happens to these problems is summarized in Figure 4. We start in the lefthand column with those respondents who report that they are faced with an important personal or family problem—a group that included most of the respondents in each of the four groups. We then divide them in the middle column into those who mention the government as an agency that could help them in dealing with this problem, and in turn divide those who do and do not see the government as a relevant source of help in dealing with their problems into those who have contacted the government on some problem and those who have not. Let us compare Blacks and whites as we move across the diagram. In the middle column we see, as was pointed out earlier in Table 21, that Blacks are more likely to mention the government as a potential

Table 24

PROPORTION LIKELY TO MAKE DEMANDS THROUGH ELITE CONTACTS,* BY RACE AND CASTE (in percentages)

Proportion Who	United States				India			
	Total	White	Black	Black R.R.**	Total	Caste-Hindus	Harijans	Harijans R.R.**
Contacted elite	30	33	14	.50	19	21	11	.59
Felt that they can contact elite directly	43	46	34	.79	30	32	24	.79
Felt that contact with elite is possible through connections	10	8	19	1.9	29	28	35	1.2
Felt they need connections but could not find them	17	13	33	1.9	22	20	31	1.4
Total %	100	100	100		100	100	100	
(n)	(2,521)	(2,260)	(261)		(2,126)	(1,776)	(350)	

*Persons who felt that they can contact elite for solving personal or community problems either indirectly through a connection or directly, and those who have contacted elites have been considered as those who are likely to "input" demands.

**R.R. is representation ratio.

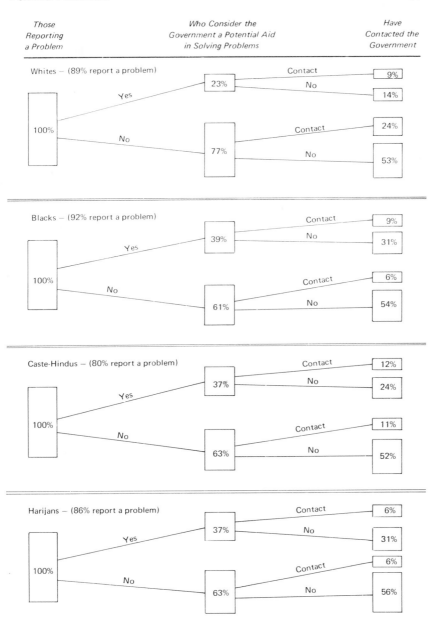

Those Reporting a Problem	Who Consider the Government a Potential Aid in Solving Problems	Have Contacted the Government

Whites — (89% report a problem)

Blacks — (92% report a problem)

Caste-Hindus — (80% report a problem)

Harijans — (86% report a problem)

Figure 4

THE FLOW FROM PROBLEMS TO CONTACT

problem solver—thirty-nine percent do in contrast with twenty-
three percent of whites. In this sense, one observes a higher degree
of political expectation among Blacks than among whites.
Compare, then, the Blacks and the whites in the far right of the
diagram. In each group, a bit over half neither expects the
government to be a relevant helper nor has contacted the
government on such a problem. But in the other categories there
are interesting differences. Nine percent of the Blacks and nine
percent of the whites both have expectations from the government
and are active; but when it comes to the interesting group that
considers the government relevant to personal problems but has
not contacted the government on such a problem, we find
fourteen percent of the whites and thirty-one percent of the
Blacks. And the similarity in proportions of the Blacks and whites
who both think the government is relevant and also have the
contacts ought not to obscure the fact that many more Blacks
than whites consider the government as the relevant institution to
help them with their problems. Thus, if we consider only those
who think the government is a relevant problem solver, we find
that a much larger percentage of that group has been active among
whites, in contrast with Blacks.

In short, a higher proportion of Blacks consider the government
relevant, but a smaller number convert this into activity. One
further comparison is interesting. Twenty-four percent of the
whites contact the government about some problem, though they
do not mention the government as the relevant problem solver for
their most pressing personal and family problems, in contrast with
six percent of the Blacks. What this suggests is that whites often
contact the government even when they do not consider the
government the relevant institution for solving their most pressing
problems—obviously enjoying the "luxury" of contacting about
problems less pressing. Thus Black contact, when it takes place, is
more likely than white contact to be on pressing problems; but it
is much less likely to take place.

The contrast between Harijans and caste-Hindus is not quite as
sharp, but it is similar. The two groups resemble each other in
terms of the proportions which consider the government a relevant
problem solver for their most pressing problems. In this sense,
both groups in India are equally politicized. But in the far right

column we see that Harijans who consider the government relevant to their problems are half as likely as caste-Hindus to have contacted the government—six percent to twelve percent. And, similar to the situation in the United States, more of the dominant group initiate contact even when the government is not considered the relevant problem solver for their most pressing problems than do the members of the deprived group.

In short, for the deprived groups, the objective problems exist, they are perceived as problems, and the government is perceived as relevant to the problems. Where the gap comes is in the conversion of these perceptions into activity.

One can take the discussion one step further. We have thus far been talking of the conditions under which individuals might contact the government and have found a greater likelihood that the dominant groups would so contact despite the fact of the somewhat greater level of need among the more deprived group. But the imbalance might go further, for we have not yet considered the result of the contact. Not only might the deprived groups contact less often, but their frequency of success might be lower. We have no measure of the success of contacts with the government, but we do have information on one aspect of such contacts that might have important implications for the nature of the results of the contact. We were interested in the type of problem that respondents reported bringing to governmental offices; in particular, in the extent to which individuals raised with governmental officials problems that referred to themselves or their family or problems referring to the larger community or society. The distinction is important for a number of theoretical reasons having to do with the extent to which the individual receives from the government, benefits that are particularized to himself and his family, or whether in his contact with the government he tries to affect more general governmental policies.

The data (reported in Table 25) are quite striking and provide both an interesting parallel between the two countries and an interesting difference between the dominant and deprived groups. If we consider only those individuals who have contacted the government, we find that Indian respondents are more likely to report that they raised an issue limited in its relevance to themselves and their immediate families, than are American

Table 25

REFERENT OF CONTACT, BY RACE AND CASTE

(contactors only; in percentages)

	United States			India		
	Total	White	Black	Total	Caste-Hindu	Harijan
Contact on a Personal or Family matter	35 (9)*	34 (10)	48 (6)	71 (14)	69 (15)	83 (9)
Contact on a Communal or Social Matter	65 (18)	66 (20)	52 (6)	25 (5)	26 (6)	17 (2)
Other Problems	—	—	—	4 (1)	5 (1)	— (—)
Total % Contactors	100	100	100	100	100	100
(n)	(778)	(743)	(35)	(412)	(373)	(39)

*The figures in parentheses are the proportion of the entire group who contact in a particular manner. For instance, the upper left cell indicates that 35% of the Americans *who contact officials* contact on a personal matter while 9% of the entire *American sample (contactors and noncontactors)* contact on such a problem.

respondents—seventy-one percent contrasted with thirty-five percent. And within each country, the deprived group is more likely to report contacts with such a narrow referent than is the dominant group. Thus thirty-four percent of the white contactors report raising a problem whose referent is limited to themselves and their family, in comparison with forty-eight percent of the Black contactors. In India, sixty-nine percent of the caste-Hindu contactors raise such a personal problem, while eighty-three percent of the Harijans do. There are a number of possible sources for this difference. It may simply reflect the greater level of need of the more deprived groups that requires that the members of those groups who manage to contact an official focus on the most immediate problems with which they are faced. In this connection, it is interesting to note that, comparing all four groups, the frequency with which those who contact focus solely on a problem particularized to themselves varies directly with the affluence of the group, Harijans are most likely to mention such a problem when contacting, caste-Hindus are next, followed by Blacks and whites. Or the difference may merely reflect a greater ability to articulate problems at a general level among more well-educated groups—those with low education being more likely to phrase general problems in personal terms and those with higher education doing the opposite. Some evidence suggests that the latter is not the case.*

Our concern here is not with the source of this difference, but with some possible consequences. If these differences in types of problems individuals report bringing to officials is a valid one, it means that officials receive different kinds of messages from the different groups. From the deprived groups, they receive messages about problems, the solutions of which aid the deprived individual (assuming a favorable response on the part of the official), but have little general impact. From the dominant group, the message is about a more general problem, the solution of which (again assuming a favorable response) has a general impact. The member of the deprived group asking for a particularized benefit does not further the cause of his group.

---

*For a fuller discussion of this general issue, see Verba and Nie (forthcoming: chs. 3 and 4).

In short, the deprived groups—and the situation is most extreme among the Blacks—have more severe problems, are more likely to see the government as the relevant problem solver, but are less likely to initiate contact about these problems. And when they do contact, the problem they bring with them tends to have a narrow referent with little potential for helping others like them. The situation is shown more clearly if we compare the figures in parenthesis in the cells of Table 25. These simply report the percentages of the four groups as a whole—not just the contactors—who have contacted on personal problems or more general social problems. In the United States, one finds that whites have contacted more frequently than Blacks on either type of problem; but the difference is most striking in terms of contact on a social problem: twenty percent of the whites as against, only six percent of the Blacks. In India, the situation is similar. Only two percent of all Harijans have contacted on a problem with a social referent; as against six percent of the caste-Hindus.

The last political activity on which we comment is cooperative activity. If there are barriers to the individual who wants to contact the government, an alternative political strategy is to work within the group; to develop it internally. And this can have two purposes. This group can become a self-help agency, in which case there need be less dependence on government. Or the group can use the great political power of numbers to further its political claims. Table 20 indicated that the Black Americans are as likely as the white Americans to engage in such activity. Harijans, in contrast, are less likely than caste-Hindus to take part in such activities. And here the difference may well be due to the social and economic characteristics that prevent the development of the internal leadership and organizational structure that would facilitate such cooperative activity. This, of course, is not inconsistent with the generally lower frequency of this kind of activity for Indians in general compared with the American. Blacks, on the other hand, have both higher levels of education and a wider range of educational levels represented in the group, plus a wider range of occupations that provide the potential leadership. They have traditionally strong institutions such as the church. And they have the advantages of shared language and shared media.

SUMMATION

We have found that the patterns of political activity are as we expected. Harijans differ least from caste-Hindus in relation to participation in elections, in particular in terms of voting. Blacks differ least from whites in organized activities. And both Blacks and Harijans are "deprived" when it comes to access to government via citizen-initiated contacts.

This merely begins our consideration of political activity. We wish to consider these activities further, to see if they are indeed equivalent activities: Is the vote the same for Harijans and for Black Americans or are we dealing with acts that seem similar but are in fact quite different? And we want to compare the degree of deprivation in politics with that in relation to other social spheres. Lastly, we want to see how different groups come to participate.

Appendix to Chapter IV

Table 26

VOTING RATES FOR BLACKS AND WHITES

(1966, Congressional Election)

	United States	White	Black
All persons of voting age (in, 000)	112,800	101,205	10,533
Persons registered (in, 000)	79,295	72,544	6,345
Percentage registered to total voting age	70	72	60
Percentage who voted to total voting age	55	57	42
Percentage who voted to total registered	79	80	69

SOURCE: U.S. Department of Commerce, *Current Population Report,* "Voting and Registration in the election of November 1966;" (1968). The figures and percentages are based on estimates done by the Census Bureau on the basis of the sample survey. For the reliability of the estimates and calculation of standard error see *ibid* pp. 8-9.

THE NATURE OF PARTICIPATION

Measures indicating frequency of participation are somewhat ambiguous. What seems to be the "same" political act may in different circumstances actually be quite different. Two individuals may vote, but their motivations or the results of the vote may be quite different though they both vote the same way (see Verba, 1969). Of particular interest to us is the relationship between political interest and political activity. Interest is the subjective side of activity; it is indexed by a series of questions on amount of political interest and frequency of political discussion. (Table 13 presented data on this.) In general, we would expect those who are most active in politics to be most interested; indeed, that political interest would be a prime cause of political activity. But this may not be the case. Activity without interest is possible.

The relationship between level of interest and level of activity is relevant from two points of view. On the one hand, the relationship between interest and activity within a group tells us something about the nature of the participation of that group. If there is, everything else being equal, a strong relationship, it suggests that the interest of the individual in politics leads him to participate. If there is little or no relationship, it suggests that the reason why individuals participate is not connected with their own subjective involvement; that they are participating out of habit, or are induced to participate by others, or expect some reward not connected with general political outcomes.

In addition, the relationship between participation and interest is important because of its impact on the nature of the participant population. We are concerned with how interested in politics is the population of a society as well as with how interested are certain subgroups: Blacks, whites, Harijans, and caste-Hindus. But of equal interest is the level of involvement of the *activist* portion of these groups. Are those who are active in political life interested and involved in the political matters of society? Are active Blacks more or less interested than active whites? The consequences of activity may be quite different depending on the other characteristics of the activities.

The level of political interest of the activist segment of a group depends upon the level of interest of that group as a whole as well as upon the relationship of participation to interest. If the level of interest of a group is generally low, but the relationship between interest and participation is high, the activist portion of that group will be highly interested, simply because only those who are most interested become active.

Tables 27 and 28 present the level of political interest for the four groups we have been considering, and the level of political interest of the activist portions of those groups. Thus we can see what the level of interest is for Blacks in general and compare this with the level of interest of the Black voting population or the Black campaign activists. This tells us something about what the activist population looks like in terms of interest. In addition, we present for each of the four groups a measure of association (Somers' D) between each of the four political activities and our scale of political involvement. One can interpret this statistic as a

Table 27

LEVELS OF INTEREST IN POLITICS AMONG THOSE WHO ARE POLITICALLY ACTIVE, BY RACE (in percentages)

| | Entire Group | | Those Who Vote | | Types of Political Activity | | | | | |
| | | | | | Those Who Participate in Campaign Activity | | Those Who Are Involved in Cooperative Activity | | Those Who Contact Elite | |
Level of Interest	White	Black	White	Black	White	Black	White	Black	White	Black
Low	22	21	14	16	6	7	6	8	8	22
Medium	44	45	44	44	35	31	37	31	42	27
High	32	33	41	40	59	62	57	60	50	51
Total %	100	100	100	100	100	100	100	100	100	100
(n)	(2,260)	(261)	(1,064)	(91)	(583)	(51)	(516)	(57)	(743)	(35)
Somers' D*			.21	.20	.39	.41	.30	.36	.35	.27

*Somers' D, asymmetric for Blacks and whites separately, with interest in politics dependent.

Table 28

LEVELS OF INTEREST IN POLITICS AMONG THOSE WHO ARE POLITICALLY ACTIVE, BY CASTE (in percentages)

| | Entire Group | | Those Who Vote | | Types of Political Activity | | | | | |
| | | | | | Those Who Participate in Campaign Activity | | Those Who Are Involved in Cooperative Activity | | Those Who Contact Elite | |
Level of Interest	Caste-Hindus	Harijans	Caste-Hindus	Harijans	Caste-Hindus	Harijans	Caste-Hindus	Harijans	Caste-Hindus	Harijans
Low	35	47	29	44	9	10	4	3	16	13
Medium	32	34	33	35	10	24	11	19	22	41
High	34	20	38	21	81	66	85	78	63	46
Total %	100	100	100	100	100	100	100	100	100	100
(n)	(1,776)	(350)	(746)	(156)	(745)	(127)	(544)	(89)	(373)	(39)
Somers' D^*			.07	.02	.35	.19	.44	.43	.40	.46

*Somers' D, asymmetric for caste-Hindu and Harijans separately, with interest in politics dependent.

measure of information. If the association between interest and some activity is close to zero, one knows nothing more about the level of political interest of an individual by knowing that he is active; in other words, activists would be no different from the rest of the population in their level of involvement.

An inspection of the tables makes several points clear: One point is that voting differs from the other political acts. For all four groups, the association between involvement and voting is substantially lower than the association of other types of activity with involvement. For Blacks and whites there is a positive association of similar magnitude (.20 and .21 for Blacks and whites respectively) between voting and involvement—that is, if an individual is a voter he is more likely to be involved, but the association is much weaker than that between any of the other activity measures and involvement. In India, there is almost no association between voting and involvement for Harijans and caste-Hindus (.02 and .07 for Harijans and caste-Hindus respectively), a situation that is different from that found in connection with the other activity measures. The association between interest and other activities is consistently high. In short, voting differs from other political acts; and it probably differs in that it requires less motivation. Many vote even if they are not much politically involved or, conversely, many who are politically involved do not vote. The contrast between voting and other political acts makes it clear that the use of the vote as an indicator of political activity in general—as it is often used—is misleading.

The difference between voting and other forms of activity— particularly in India—is reinforced if one compares the relationship between political information and voting with the relationship between information and the other political acts. For Harijans and caste-Hindus, the measure of association (Somers' D) between our measure of information and voting is .06 and .08 respectively; while the associations between information and the other three activities range between .28 and .40. The association between information and campaign activity is .28 for Harijans and .36 for caste-Hindus; between cooperative activity and information, .32 for Harijans and .38 for caste-Hindus; and the association between contacting and information .40 for Harijans and .36 for caste-Hindus.* In other words, voters are a little more informed than the population as a whole, but only a little. Other activists differ much more from the nonactivists in information level.

In addition to the difference between voting and other political acts, there is an interesting difference between the countries. In the United States, Blacks are generally similar to whites in the association of interest and participation. (The major difference is in relation to contacting, where there is a closer association between interest and activity for whites than for Blacks.) If we can infer a motivational basis for activity from these associations, we can say that for both groups, subjective involvement in politics plays the same positive role in political participation. In India, the situation is different. In relation to activities within the electoral process—voting and campaign activity—the association between interest and activity is lower for Harijans than for caste-Hindus. In relation to voting, the association is zero for Harijans and relatively low for caste-Hindus. This means that one knows nothing more about the level of interest of a Harijan by knowing that he votes—as can be seen by comparing the distribution into those with high, medium, and low involvement for all Harijans with that for voting Harijans. Thus forty-seven percent of the Harijans have no interest whatever in politics (as measured on our scale); and, since there is no association between voting and level of involvement, a quite similar percentage of the Harijan *voters* (forty-four percent) have no political interest.

When it comes to campaign activity, one finds a positive association between activity and involvement for Harijans but not as close as that for caste-Hindus. Thus Harijan campaign activists are more likely to be politically involved than are those who are not active, but not to the same extent as with caste-Hindus. On the other hand, when we turn to the other two modes of activity—cooperative activity and contacting—we find a similarity between the two groups in terms of the relationship of the activity with involvement.

---

*The similarity between Harijans and caste-Hindus in the association between information and the several modes of activity suggests that our measure of information—about which we expressed some doubts—may be quite valid.

The comparison of the relationships of interest to activity across the four kinds of activities is fascinating from a number of points of view. In the first place it indicates why one must be cautious in comparing absolute levels of activity without attempting to obtain some information as to the nature or meaning of the activity from the point of view of the activist. In those types of activity where the absolute level of participation on the part of Harijans is most similar to the level of participation among the dominant group (activity within the electoral process), the association between activity and interest (and, inferentially, the motivational basis of the activity) is most different between the two groups. Where the difference in level of activity between Harijans and caste-Hindus is most severe—cooperative activity and contacting—the association between the activity and interest is most similar between the deprived and dominant groups.

Substantively, the data for India suggest that within the electoral process, Harijans are more mobilized from without than from within. They are more likely to take part without any strong internal motivational basis. In connection with the other forms of activity where they are least likely to be active, those who are active are active on the basis of the same internal motivation that inspires the caste-Hindus. The data cannot be taken to mean that Harijans are passively manipulated by other castes for the benefit of others. It may not be that unmotivated voting (if we can assume that is what we are observing) is ineffectual voting; that depends on many other characteristics, not merely on the motivational basis of the vote. And to say that the evidence is that Harijan voting is externally motivated is to say that it is external to the individual Harijan. He is seemingly not motivated by his *own* involvement in politics, but this does not mean that the external mobilizers—if such there be—are necessarily from outside the Harijan community. However, the coupling of the low rate of cooperative activity among Harijans with the higher rate of electoral activity suggests that those Harijans who are active tend to work through groups led by others, rather than by Harijans.

The nature of Harijan voting is made clearer if we look at Table 29. This table takes the same form as the previous except that level of partisanship replaces the level of interest as the subjective measure in whose association with activity we are concerned. And the activities that we deal with are those in the electoral

Table 29

DEGREE OF PARTISANSHIP AMONG THOSE WHO ARE POLITICALLY ACTIVE, BY RACE AND CASTE (in percentages)

	United States						India					
Level of Partisanship	All Whites	All Blacks	White Voters	Black Voters	White Campaign Activist	Black Campaign Activist	All Caste-Hindus	All Harijans	Caste-Hindu Voters	Harijan Voters	Caste-Hindu Campaign Activist	Harijan Campaign Activist
Independents	8	4	6	0	4	1	32	44	25	26	8	9
Weak partisan	14	12	13	13	16	11	10	5	7	8	5	7
Moderate partisan	44	35	41	29	36	22	14	10	14	11	10	8
Strong partisan	35	50	41	58	45	66	44	41	55	55	78	76
Total %	100	100	100	100	100	100	100	100	100	100	100	100
(n)	(2,260)	(261)	(1,064)	(91)	(583)	(51)	(1,776)	(350)	(746)	(156)	(745)	(127)
Somers' D**			.18	.16	.11	.14			.19	.27	.30	.19

*For a definition of the partisan type, see Table 15.

**Somers' D between partisanship and activity for each of the groups, with partisanship dependent.

process—voting and campaign activity. The data show that for all four groups there is an association between partisanship and electoral activity. If you know a man is a voter or a campaign activist, you know that he is more likely to be a strong partisan. What is interesting on the table is the fairly close association between voting and partisanship for Harijans. Though the Harijan voter is no more involved in politics—that is, has no more interest or engages in no more discussion—than the nonvoter, the Harijan voter is much more likely to be a partisan. Thus, we saw that forty-seven percent of all Harijans had no interest in politics, and forty-four percent of the Harijan voters had no interest. But forty-four percent of the Harijans express no party affiliation while only twenty-six percent of the Harijan voters are unaffiliated. If this association allows an inference about motivation, we may say that attachment to a party motivates Harijan voting; general political involvement does not. And this contrast between partisanship and general political involvement is true, though to a lesser extent, for caste-Hindus. (The greater strength of association of partisanship with activity in India than in the United States—for dominant and deprived groups—is also striking. We will return to that point.)

The contrast with American Blacks is also striking here. Though, for American Blacks, other forms of activity are more closely associated with interest than is voting, there is, nevertheless, in contrast with Harijans, a positive association between voting and interest—an association as strong as that found for whites. Blacks we have suggested may be politically motivated by a sense of group consciousness; an awareness of their specially deprived position that can form the basis of political activity. Harijans, on the other hand, may be inhibited from developing this consciousness by the low absolute level of their education and the dispersed nature of the group. One measure of group consciousness is the frequency with which individuals, in response to open questions, refer to racial or caste matters. Thus on our interview we asked a number of open questions, in response to which individuals could mention, if they wished, race or caste. In the United States, these were questions on the major personal, community, and national problems perceived by the respondent, as well as a question on the major conflicts in the community (the latter was reported earlier in Table 16). The number of times race was referred to in answer to these questions—conflict between Blacks and whites was cited or reference made to a major problem having to do with race relations—becomes our scale of group consciousness for Blacks. In India, a similar measure of group consciousness was based on a question about the groups involved in community conflict and a question about the most influential group within the community. Again, the frequency of mention of caste groupings by Harijans was considered a measure of group consciousness. In Table 30 we compare various kinds of activists with the whole group in terms of group consciousness and show the association between group consciousness and participation. For one thing, there is more frequent group consciousness among Blacks than among Harijans. Comparing the first columns, we find that sixty-three percent of blacks mention race in answer to our question in comparison with thirty-one percent of Harijans who mention caste.*

For Blacks there is an association between most forms of activity and group consciousness. Black voting is associated with group consciousness; Black voters are more likely to mention race in response to our open questions than are Blacks in general. Sixty-three percent of all Blacks mention race, compared with seventy-five percent of Black voters. Almost no such association is found for Harijans; thirty-two percent of all Harijans mention caste in comparison with thirty-five percent of Harijan voters. (The association between group consciousness and voting for Blacks is .16; for Harijans is .03.) The situation in relation to voting differs from that in relation to campaign activity. Campaign activity is associated with group consciousness for both Blacks and

*The Black group consciousness scale is built on the basis of more questions—i.e., Blacks had more opportunities to mention race. But the reason we did not use these additional questions—questions about personal, communal, or national problems—for the group consciousness scale in India was simply that caste was almost never mentioned in answering them. The addition of these questions would not have changed the results.

Questions about major problems were also asked in India, but economic needs so overwhelmed the answers that there were few mentions of caste in the answers.

Table 30

GROUP CONSCIOUSNESS OF BLACK
AND HARIJAN ACTIVISTS (in percentages)

Group Consciousness	All Blacks	Black Voters	Black Campaign Activists	Black Coopera- ative Activists	Black Con- tactors
Frequency of mention of race:					
No mention	38	24	11	23	31
Once	38	45	46	49	47
Two or more	25	30	43	28	22
Total %	100	100	100	100	100
(n)	(261)	(91)	(51)	(57)	(35)
Somers' D*		.16	.25	.12	.01

Group Consciousness	All Harijans	Harijan Voters	Harijan Campaign Activists	Harijan Coopera- tive Activists	Harijan Con- tactors
Frequency of mention of caste:					
No mention	68	64	52	55	66
Once	27	30	32	34	22
Two or more	5	5	16	11	11
Total %	100	100	100	100	100
(n)	(350)	(156)	(127)	(89)	(64)
Somers' D**		.03	.22	.05	.03

*Somers' D between group consciousness and activity for Blacks only.

**Somers' D between group consciousness and activity for Harijans.

Harijans. The association is similar for Blacks and Harijans (.25 and .22 respectively) and is for each group the strongest association between group consciousness and an activity. In other words, a much smaller number of Harijans engages in campaign activity or is group conscious than among Blacks, but the variables "work" the same way; the more group conscious they are, the more they are active. When we compare this association with the situation in relation to voting, it reinforces our interpretation of Harijan voting as an externally motivated act not deriving from the internalized beliefs of the individual.*

We can look at the data just presented from another point of view: in terms of the resultant characteristics of the participants. As pointed out above, the "quality" of the participant population depends upon the interest and information levels of the population as a whole and the selection process (equivalent to the statistical association) between the subjective state and the activity. If the level of information, for instance, is low in a particular group, and there is no association between information level and a particular activity, the activists from that group will also have low levels of information. On the other hand, if the information level of a group is low, but there is a close association between an activity and information—that is, those who are active come disproportionately from the more informed members of that group—the activist portion of that group will be relatively well informed.

Table 31 presents data on the information and interest levels of the activist portions of our four groups. The data presented are the proportion of the activist group that is low on interest or on information. For example, the figure in the far upper left of the table means that fourteen percent of the white voters are low in political interest, the figure on the right of the top row means that

*For Harijans, there is little association between group consciousness and either contact or cooperative activity; for Blacks, an association exists between cooperative activity and group consciousness, but not between contact and group consciousness. Contact tends, however, to be a rather nonpolitical activity involving requests for specific family or personal benefits. On this general topic see Sidney Verba and Norman Nie (forthcoming).

Table 31

UNINTERESTED AND UNINFORMED ACTIVISTS:
PROPORTION UNINTERESTED OR UNINFORMED IN
VARIOUS ACTIVIST POPULATIONS (in percentages)

	Among Voters Who Are:			
Percentage Who Are:	*White (1,064)* *	*Black (91)*	*Caste-Hindu (746)*	*Harijan (156)*
Low in interest	14	16	29	44
Low in information	7	20	43	63

	Among Campaign Activists Who Are:			
Percentage Who Are:	*White (583)*	*Black (51)*	*Caste-Hindu (745)*	*Harijan (127)*
Low in interest	6	7	9	10
Low in information	8	24	11	20

	Among Cooperative Activists Who Are:			
Percentage Who Are:	*White (516)*	*Black (57)*	*Caste-Hindu (544)*	*Harijan (89)*
Low in interest	6	8	4	3
Low in information	7	13	7	34

	Among Contactors Who Are:			
Percentage Who Are:	*White (743)*	*Black (135)*	*Caste-Hindu (373)*	*Harijan (39)*
Low in interest	8	22	16	13
Low in information	9	19	24	36

*The n of each type in parentheses.

forty-four percent of the Harijan voters are low in interest. There is one difference in the data reported for Indian respondents and American respondents: In India, the low category of interest or information can be interpreted as a "none" category—that is, we report data on those who have no interest in politics and engage in no political discussion, and on those who could answer none of the information questions we asked. In the United States, we have adopted a somewhat less stringent criterion, since so few respondents were in this absolutely low category. The uninvolved are those who fall in the lowest quartile of the involvement scale. This means that they may report some interest or some discussion, but not much. The uninformed in the United States are those who could answer no more than two of the eight information questions we asked (eighteen percent of the population falls in this category).

Table 31 contains a lot of information relevant to differences among the various political acts, differences between interest and information, and differences among the four groups. Let us first consider the proportion of activists who are subjectively interested in politics—that is, who take part but do not express general concern with political matters. (These are in the top rows of each subsection of the table.) The first point that may be made is that the proportion of uninterested activists is higher for voting than for the other acts. The only exception is for Blacks, where the proportion of uninterested contactors is greater than the proportion of uninterested voters,* but all other comparisons of the proportion of activists who are uninvolved show that the uninvolved voters are found two or more times as frequently as are uninterested campaign, cooperative or contacting activists (twelve comparisons in all, of which eleven support the general finding).

If one compares across the countries, several points about the distinction between voting and the other acts emerge. In relation to voting there is both a difference between the countries, with a larger proportion of uninterested voters in India (and the

---

*Contacting, for Blacks especially, tends to be relatively "nonpolitical" activity—that is, it often relates to specific personal and family problems. For an extended discussion, see Verba and Nie (forthcoming).

difference would be greater if we used as stringent a criterion of noninterest in the United States as we use in India). And whereas there is little difference between Blacks and whites in the United States, there is a sharp difference between Harijans and caste-Hindus in the proportion of voters who are uninterested. Thus the proportions of voters who are uninterested are sixteen and fourteen percent respectively for Blacks and whites in the United States; and forty-four and twenty-nine percent for the Harijans and caste-Hindus in India. But in relation to the other measures of activity, there is little difference between the United States and India, and little difference between the dominant and deprived groups within each country. (With the exception of contact in the United States; see footnote page 152.) Uninterested activists are rare in both countries and in both groups in each country.

The data on information (the second row in each section of the table) take a somewhat different shape from those on interest. The data for the United States differ from those for India again largely in relation to the vote. Uninformed voting is quite frequent in India among both the Harijans and caste-Hindus, though more frequent among the former. And it is more frequent than is uninformed campaign activity or cooperative activity or contacting. In the United States, there is little difference between voting and the other activities in the frequency with which we find activists who are uninformed.

The data for uninformed activists differ from those on uninterested activists in one respect. For information, we find a cross-national uniformity whereby the activists of the deprived group are less informed than the activists of the dominant group. Thus, whereas Black activists were in general as interested in politics as were white activists, and Harijan activists were, with the exception of voting, as interested as caste-Hindus, we find that Black and Harijan activists are less informed than are white or caste-Hindu activists in relation to every mode of activity. What this means is that when one looks beyond the vote—and particularly when one looks at campaign and cooperative activity—one finds few individuals from either dominant or deprived groups who are activists but uninterested in politics. For information, the situation differs. Few activists from the dominant group are uninformed, while a much larger proportion of the activists from the deprived groups are uninformed.

The interpretation of the data is somewhat uncertain. The distinction between the proportion of uninformed voters and uninformed campaigners, cooperative activists, or contactors in India adds confirmation to our view that voting—particularly in India—is an act different from the others. And since this involves comparisons between Harijans as voters and Harijans as campaigners, and other similar comparisons within the subgroups, we are not faced with the ambiguity of the information variable for distinguishing between nations or among groups. The uniform difference one finds between dominant and deprived groups in terms of the proportion of uninformed activists is harder to interpret, since it may reflect a process of political mobilization of deprived groups that is unaccompanied by the skills which would accompany political activity deriving from increased education and other changes in social status. Or it may simply be, as suggested earlier, that the questions asked are more relevant to the dominant than to the deprived groups. But in either case the result may be the same; the activist members of deprived groups are as informed about the dominant political system as are the activists of the dominant groups.

Thus far, our data for India are consistent—or largely consistent—with our expectations as to the types of political activity we would find between the two groups. Harijans appear to be a type of political group whose activity—at least in the electoral sphere (and particularly in relation to voting) where they are most active—does not derive from internal motivation, but perhaps from partisan mobilization. The relationship between interest and electoral activity (voting and campaigning) is weak or nonexistent for them; that between voting and group consciousness is weak; but the relationship between partisanship and electoral activity is strong. The group most similar to them in this respect are the caste-Hindus, though their electoral activity is accompanied by more interest and information than is that among the Harijans. But the data do suggest that electoral activity in India is an activity for which a good deal of the impetus is external to the participant.

**Race, Caste and Participation in
Traditional and Nontraditional Settings**

One of the crucial conclusions suggested by the data thus far is that Harijan electoral activity is externally mobilized. For other kinds of activity, Harijan activism is much rarer, but the motivational basis is the same as that of caste-Hindus. If this is the case, we would expect Harijan electoral activity to be highest in settings where traditional deferential relationships are stronger, since this would enhance external mobilization; while the activity deriving from internalized motivation would be more likely found in less traditional settings. Consider the data in Table 32. This table compares the activity rates of the deprived and dominant groups in more traditional settings (rural areas in India, the South in the United States) and in less traditional settings (urban areas in India and the non-South in the United States). The figures are the simple difference in the activity rates between Harijans and caste-Hindus or between Blacks and whites. Negative percentages mean that the deprived group participates that much less than the dominant group—for instance, the voting turnout in rural areas is one percent lower for Harijans than for caste-Hindus. Our main concern is not with the magnitude of deprivation in either the traditional or the nontraditional sector, but with a comparison between the two sectors in terms of where the magnitude of deprivation is greater.

In India, the data are generally consistent with our hypothesis that electoral activity is more characteristic of rural than urban Harijans. For voting, there is little difference between Harijan and caste-Hindu turnout in either setting. Despite the more "traditional" place they would hold in rural areas and the consequent inhibitions to participation that one might expect, Harijans are no worse off in relation to voting in rural areas than in urban areas. And in connection with campaign activity, we find them as active as caste-Hindus in the rural areas, but less active in the urban; in other words, we find them better off in rural than in urban areas when it comes to campaign activity. For cooperative

Table 32

DIFFERENCE IN DEPRIVED AND DOMINANT
GROUP ACTIVITY RATES IN TRADITIONAL
AND NONTRADITIONAL SETTINGS* (in percentages)

Types of Activity	India		United States	
	Rural	*Urban*	*South*	*Non-South*
Voting	− 1**	− 1	−11	− 5
Campaign activity	− 1	−11	− 4	− 6
Cooperative activity	− 7	+ 8	+ 2	− 5
Contacting	−10	0	−19	−16

*Figures are: Percentage active among deprived group *minus* the percentage active among dominant group. A negative percentage means that the deprived group is that much less active on that measure; a positive percentage that they are more active.

**Numbers: Harijan, rural (280); Caste-Hindu, rural (1,164); Harijan, urban (71); Caste-Hindu, urban (615); Blacks, South (215); whites, South (755); Blacks, North (190); whites, North (1,857).

and contacting activity, the pattern is reversed. Harijans are less active than caste-Hindus in rural settings but as active (contacting) or more active (cooperative activity) in urban settings. Thus, those electoral activities where Harijan activism is not associated with subjective involvement are more characteristic of rural Harijans. Those nonelectoral activities where Harijan activism is associated with subjective involvement are more characteristic of urban Harijans—a result consistent with our hypothesis that Harijan electoral activity is mobilized from outside the individual.

In the United States, the patterns are somewhat more complex. Blacks are relatively less active in the traditional setting (the South) in voting and, to a lesser extent, in contact. On the other hand, when it comes to cooperative activity and (to a slight degree) campaign activity, they are relatively better off in the South. On cooperative activity, they are a bit more active than whites in the South and a bit less active in the non-South. The comparison is intriguing. The lower voting rate in the South has historical roots, while the lower rate of contacting local officials in the South than in the non-South probably reflects the greater height of the ascriptive boundaries there. On the other hand, southern Black activity seems of a highly organized, elite rather than mass, kind; there is in a sense more campaign activity than mass voting, more cooperative activity than individual contacts.

Among Harijans, one has the impression of a group externally mobilized—especially in the rural areas in relation to electoral activity. Among Blacks, especially in the South, one gets the impression of a greater leadership activity with a somewhat lagging mass base.

Chapter VII

RACE/CASTE, CLASS AND POLITICS

Thus far we have discussed the relative positions of Blacks and Harijans in the economic systems of their societies and in the political systems. We have compared their occupations, income, and education with that of the dominant groups, and we have compared their rates of political behavior. We have also attempted to interpret the meaning of that political behavior by considering, in Chapter VI, the orientational characteristics that accompany such behavior. But the more interesting questions involve not the position of the deprived groups within the economic and the political systems, but the relationship of these positions to one another.

In making this connection, we are really considering the relationship among three hierarchies in society—the ascriptive status hierarchy reflected in race and caste, the hierarchy of social class (involving nonascriptive characteristics such as education, income, and occupational level), and a political hierarchy (involving amount of political access, participation, and power). The study of the relationship between political position and position on other hierarchies is particularly interesting in relation to ascriptive groups such as Blacks and Harijans because of the supposed diffuseness of their status. In the ideal caste-dominated society, each of the individual's positions—his economic position, his positions in terms of political power, in terms of ritual respect, in terms of access to facilities, and so forth—is systematically linked to his caste position. Modern society, on the other hand, involves more specific relations; the individual operates in independent spheres not all determined by his single overriding caste or kinship position. In the former system, all the statuses of an individual, because they are dominated by the one caste status, would be congruent. The ideal model of total congruence among static status hierarchies—where those who are in the lowest position in terms of ritual purity are and remain the lowest in terms of economic and political position—did not in fact hold even for India before independence. Some groups were differentially ranked: Brahmins might be higher on ritual criteria, but Rajputs higher on political power; and movement of subcastes within the social hierarchy was possible (Srinivas, 1962; Sinha, 1967). Nor was the position of Blacks ever that well defined and static. But Blacks and Harijans represent those groups to which the static caste model best applies. Caste as a determinant of generalized status operates more powerfully for those at the very top and bottom of the status hierarchy, and probably most for the latter. The Brahmin remains a high-status person even if not wealthy; the Harijan or Black may remain an outcaste even if in a high educational or professional position (de Vos and Wagatsuma, 1966; Isaacs, 1964). In light of the diffusely deprived status of the "outcaste," a disjunction in the degree of change within different arenas becomes most important. This, by definition, shatters the diffuseness of the earlier situation. And in this, the political arena may be most important. It may be that the political arena is more amenable to manipulation and use by the deprived groups for a number of reasons. One of these is the dominant egalitarian ideology and the greater need for public justification for actions. This forces a closer congruence between egalitarian ideology and actual behavior in the political arena than elsewhere. In addition, the political arena is particularly open to geographically clustered groups with a high sense of identity. In India, the political arena is also open for the deprived group by fiat from the top down. Explicit compensatory measures—reserving seats for Harijans in the national and state legislatures, in the Indian Civil Service, in universities—place the Harijans on a footing of political equality that they may not necessarily have otherwise. Data to be reported below will suggest that political opportunities for movement upward may exceed economic ones. But the question remains: What next? Will improvement in the political realm lead to a change in economic status and in the set of ritual and social barriers that place Harijans and Blacks into a separate outcaste category?

The answer to the question lies in the future. If greater political opportunities are open, they may lead to successful advance or they may not. In this chapter, we will look more closely at some of the relationships across the three hierarchies. We will deal with two questions. The first has to do with the extent to which the low socioeconomic position of the deprived groups (described in Chapter III) inhibits their political participation. Or put another way, is it "being Black" or "being a Harijan" that inhibits political participation? Or is it one's low level of education? The second question is: Are the political or the economic arenas more open to the deprived groups? We ought to stress that we have, for neither question, definitive answers. But the data are illuminating.

Participation: Race, Caste and Class

The first question can be answered most quickly and simply. The difference in participation rates between the deprived and dominant groups is relatively small to begin with (as was discussed in Chapter V) and disappears when one controls for a composite measure of socioeconomic status—a measure made up of family income, educational level and occupation. These data are reported in Table 33.* In the United States, the relatively low relationship between activity and race either disappears or, in the case of cooperative activity where Blacks and whites were no different, turns negative. That is, Blacks are more likely to engage in cooperative activities than are whites when one controls for the difference in socioeconomic status. Only the difference between Blacks and whites in rates of contacting the government remains to distinguish the two groups, a result consistent with our speculation about the role of ascriptive barriers in inhibiting face-to-face contact with government officials. But even here the relationship is reduced. And in India, the situation is the same. What are quite weak relationships between Harijan status versus caste-Hindu status and participation reduce to zero.

One caution ought to be introduced in interpreting these findings. The data suggest that the underlying causal reason for the somewhat reduced rates of political activity among Blacks and Harijans lies in their socioeconomic positions, not in their birth positions as members of a deprived caste or racial group. That statement ought not to be interpreted to mean that race or caste are unimportant vis-à-vis political participation. (Just as a similar finding that the underlying causal reasons for lower school achievement was not inherent in race or caste but derives from lower family economic status does not imply race or caste are unimportant.) It is the conjunction of lower socioeconomic position with a particular ascriptive position that creates the social problems in both countries. Blacks may participate somewhat less because they are of lower education, not because they are Black, but the fact remains that it is the Black group that participates less.

One can take the subject one step further, though. We have seen that it is a set of achieved characteristics like education and income rather than race or caste per se that inhibits political participation of the deprived groups. One can now look within the various groups to see what role these achieved characteristics play

---

*The coefficients are Pearson's r. These give results quite similar in magnitude and in pattern across the various acts to Somers' D—a more appropriate measure of association (see Table 35 below for the comparable data). The Pearson coefficients allow us more easily to control for socioeconomic status.

Table 33

RELATIONSHIP OF RACE AND CASTE WITH PARTICIPATION: CONTROLLING FOR SOCIAL CLASS

Participation	Race and Participation		Caste and Participation	
	Simple r	Partial r (controlling for socio-economic status)	Simple r	Partial r (controlling for socio-economic status)
General participation*	.08	−.04	.11	−.02
Voting	.08	.00	−.04	−.02
Campaign activity	.07	−.03	.07	−.03
Cooperative activity	.00	−.10	.09	−.01
Contacting	.15	.08	.10	.01

Coefficient is Pearson's r.

*For a discussion of the measures of socioeconomic level and of participation in general, see Appendix.

within these groups. In the previous analysis where the impact of social class on the relationship between race and caste on the one hand and participation on the other were partialled out, the implicit assumption was that social class plays the same role in relation to participation for both deprived and dominant groups. However, the relationships may not be statistically additive. Rather, there may be an interaction effect such that the effect of class on participation differs substantially for the various groups. This, indeed, is one of our expectations, as spelled out earlier.

Earlier we distinguished between those participants whose activity derived from their socioeconomic position and those whose activity derived from an internal sense of group consciousness. In the former case, participation would be related to socioeconomic position and be mediated by increased involvement and information. In the latter case, involvement and participation would derive not from the individual's socioeconomic position—his amount of education or his job status—but rather from his position within the group. American whites, it was argued, are in the former category; Blacks, in the latter. In India, we argued that Harijans have many of the characteristics such as deprivation that make them analogous to Blacks, but that their absolute lower level of social and economic position and their dispersed internal structure inhibit the development of group consciousness. Thus they are less likely to be mobilized out of consciousness as a group.

The data in Table 34 are relevant to this argument. They compare the participation rates among upper- and lower-educated individuals in each of our four groups. What we are interested in is the extent to which education is related to participation. The results show a striking distinction between Blacks on the one hand and all the other groups. For all modes of activity, there is little or no difference between upper- and lower-educated Blacks in terms of rates of participation. For whites and for both Indian groups, there is a substantial difference between the upper- and lower-educated groups in terms of rates of activity—with the exception of voting in India which, as our earlier data indicate, is for both groups an externally motivated act. But for every other comparison between upper and lower education, the upper-educated group is two or more times as likely to be active. The

Table 34

PROPORTIONS ACTIVE AMONG UPPER AND LOWER EDUCATED (in percentages)

Active	Blacks		Whites		Hindus		Caste-Hindus	
	Less than High School Graduate	High School Graduate	Less than High School Graduate	High School Graduate	No Education	Some Education	No Education	Some Education
Percentage who vote	38	37	42	52	44	43	42	45
Percentage who are campaign activists	17	15	14	27	27	56	23	44
Percentage who are cooperators	12	15	12	21	14	39	14	33
Percentage who contact	13	18	24	41	8	35	12	35
(n)	(178)	(83)	(1,023)	(1,282)	(270)	(80)	(783)	(993)

data are thus consistent with the view of Blacks as having group-motivated participation rather than socioeconomically motivated participation.

Figure 5 gives greater detail on the role of education in relation to participation for the four groups. The figure reports the mean level of participation for various educational levels among our four basic population groups. The measure of participation is a general participation scale made up of all items of participation except voting (see Appendix for a description). The height of the various bars represents the mean activity level for that group. The width of the bars represent the proportions of various educational levels of the entire group. Thus the upper lefthand bar indicates that the mean level of activity for caste-Hindus with no education is .7 on the general activity scale, and that caste-Hindus with no education make up fifty-eight percent of all caste-Hindus. In addition to the mean level of activity for each group, we indicate the "gain" from education as one moves from one educational level to the next—i.e., the difference in the means between the two levels, indicated by the figures on the sloping broken lines between the bars.

Below the bar graphs relevant to each group, we report that group's mean score on the overall participation scale. The mean participation level of the various groups reflects the general findings reported in Chapter V. The deprived groups participate less than do the dominant. In the United States, the mean score on the participation scale is 2.12 for whites and 1.66 for Blacks. In India, the mean score for caste-Hindus is 1.28; for Harijans, .83. At the present moment we are not interested in the comparison of these means, but in looking within each group at the relationship between education and the mean level of participation.

The graphs for the various groups make clear the expected finding that increase in educational level is associated with an increase in political activity. For all four groups in the two countries, those with the highest level of education (beyond primary education in India and beyond secondary in the United States) are the most active politically and are substantially more active than those on the lowest levels. The one exception to the rule of increased participation with increased education is the comparison between Blacks who have not completed high school and those who have. The educational step from the former to the latter does not appear to be accompanied by increased political activity. These data are consistent with the data in Table 33 on the relative lack of association between education and participation for Blacks compared with whites, and in turn with the interpretation of the diminished role of social class in leading to participation for self-conscious groups. But the data in Figure 5 also indicate that education does play a role for Blacks at the extreme ends. There is a distinction at the lower end between the participation rates of those who did not get beyond eighth grade and those who have some high school and, more so, at the upper end between those who graduate from high school and those who have some college training.

In Table 35 we summarize the overall impact of education on the participation rates of the four groups. But we make an important distinction between "individual" gain in participation rate that accompanies education and the "group" gain:

(1) The "individual" gain from education represents the difference in mean activity level between those in the lowest educational group and those in the highest.

(2) The "group" gain from education represents the gain in participation level as one moves from the lowest to the highest education level, weighted by the number of people who "take advantage" of that gain.

The individual gain is equivalent to the difference in the height of the bars in Figure 5. The group gain takes into account the total area of the bar—i.e., both the height and the width of the bar, the latter reflecting the size of the relevant educational group.

Thus, the difference in average participation rate is 1.0 between those with no education and those with some education for caste-Hindus and 1.3 for Harijans. But many more caste-Hindus "take advantage" of that gain because twenty-one percent of the caste-Hindus have some education in contrast with thirteen percent of the Harijans. Similarly, twenty-one percent of the caste-Hindus "take advantage" of the 1.5 gain in mean participation that comes with obtaining education beyond primary school (rather than no education) whereas only four percent of the Harijans take advantage of that gain.* In short, the

---

*The computation of the "group" gain is made simply by multiplying the proportion of a group in a particular educational level above the lowest by the difference between its participation rate and the rate of those who are in the lowest educational level.

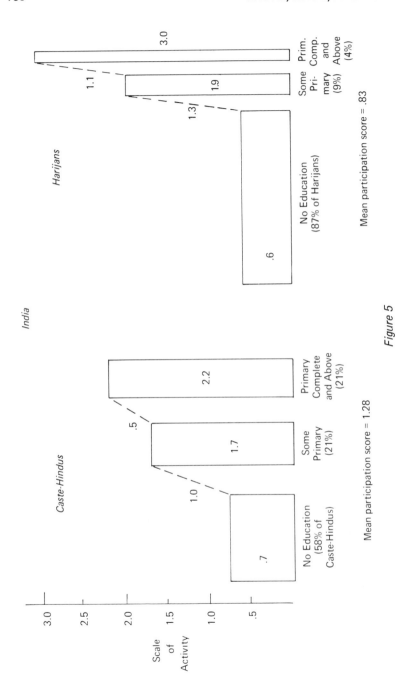

Figure 5

MEAN LEVEL OF PARTICIPATION OF VARIOUS EDUCATIONAL LEVELS

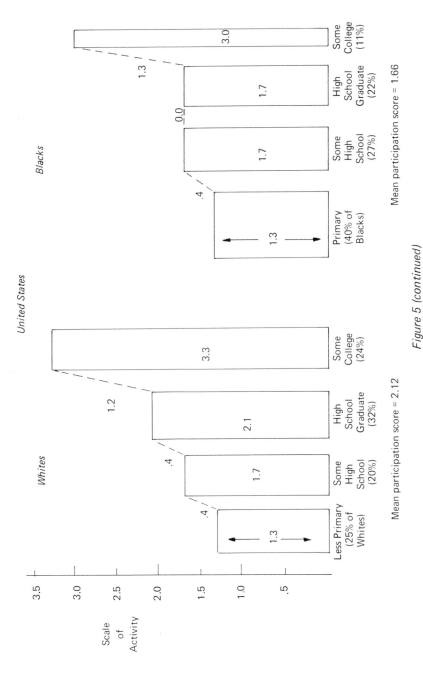

Mean participation score = 2.12   Mean participation score = 1.66

Figure 5 (continued)

MEAN LEVEL OF PARTICIPATION OF VARIOUS EDUCATIONAL LEVELS

Table 35

INDIVIDUAL AND GROUP GAINS FROM EDUCATION

Group	Gain	
	Individual	*Group*
United States:		
Whites	2.0	.82
Blacks	1.7	.38
India:		
Caste-Hindus	1.5	.52
Harijans	2.4	.21

"individual" gain from education reflects how much *individual* members of a particular group participate at higher levels of education. The "group" gain measures the amount that participation increases *for the group as a whole* by taking into account the numbers in the group who actually obtain higher educational levels. The figures are not easily comparable across the countries since the lowest and highest educational categories differ. But they are comparable within the countries.

If we consider the individual gains from education, we see a contrast between India and the United States. In India, the individual gain is greater for Harijans than for caste-Hindus. Education seems a more potent force pushing toward participation for the Harijan who obtains it than for the caste-Hindu. In contrast, the individual gain in participation rate is greater for whites than it is for Blacks—though the difference is not as great as the difference (in the other direction) in India. Again, this is consistent with our expectation that much of Black political behavior derives from other than the ordinary socioeconomic processes that lead to participation.

If we turn to the "group" gain in participation, we see the other side of the coin. In both countries the group gain is more than twice as great for the dominant group. The reason is quite simple—as reflected in the relative width of the bars in Figure 5. Many more of the dominant groups acquire higher education and, therefore, take advantage of the "gain" in participation that comes from that higher education.

Using the same general approach, we can compare the groups in terms of the individual and the group gains that come from each step upward in the educational process. The individual gain is simply the difference in the mean level of participation between those at adjacent levels of education; the group gain is the individual gain weighted by the proportion of the group who can take advantage of the gain by being at the higher educational level. Figure 5 showed us that in the United States the greatest individual gain in participation rates comes with the achievement of some college education, and that this is true for both Blacks and whites. In India, the first educational step—from no education to some—appears more important (at least for caste-Hindus) than the next from primary to post-primary. But, to repeat, one cannot easily compare across the countries on these figures since, the educational steps we are dealing with differ from country to country.

More interesting is the comparison within each nation between the individual and the group gains (see Table 36). The figures underline the conclusion from Table 35. Consider the step from high school graduation to some college education in the United States (the far right column in Table 36). The individual gain figures indicate that for Blacks and whites, this step has roughly equal payoff in terms of increased participation. But because the proportion of whites who take that step is more than twice as great as the proportion of Blacks (twenty-four percent versus eleven percent in our sample), the group gain in participation is twice as great for whites. The Indian data are even more striking. The educational step from primary educational level to post-primary is associated with an individual gain in participation rate that is twice as great for Harijans as for caste-Hindus. But because so many fewer Harijans take that step, the group gain for Harijans is less than half as great.

The data illustrate a major point we have previously made: participation, insofar as it depends upon socioeconomic status, is "stacked against" deprived groups. Those who need it most—the deprived—participate less because of that deprivation. This interpretation is best illustrated by the comparison between Harijans and caste-Hindus reported in Table 35. Education has a great impact on both groups and a greater one on Harijans. But the proportions of Harijans with higher levels of education is much smaller than those of the caste-Hindus. Thus the former would participate as much, even more, if they had the education. But the problem is that they do not have it, and the greater advantages accrue to the dominant group.

Political and Socioeconomic Deprivation, a Suggestive Comparison

We have suggested above a variety of reasons why one would expect the political system to be more "open" to ascriptively deprived groups than would the economic or the social system—that opportunities for political participation and opportunities to acquire political power or influence would be more

Table 36
INDIVIDUAL AND GROUP GAINS FROM MOVEMENT ACROSS EACH EDUCATIONAL LEVEL

United States

Group		Primary to Some High School	High School to High School Graduate	High School Graduation to Some College
Individual Gains	Whites	.4	.4	1.2
	Blacks	.4	.0	1.3
Group Gains	Whites	.08	.13	.29
	Blacks	.11	.0	.14

India

		No Education to Some	Primary to Secondary
Individual Gains	Caste-Hindus	1.0	.5
	Harijans	1.3	1.1
Group Gain	Caste-Hindus	.21	.10
	Harijans	.11	.04

equal than opportunities for jobs, income, or education. But is
this, in fact, the case? Such a question allows of no precise answer.
One of the reasons is that one is comparing different hierarchies
measured by different variables. How many dollars or rupees of
income is a vote worth? Votes or other acts of participation are
opportunities to acquire other benefits, but how much, if
anything, they bring is uncertain.

Nevertheless, because our concern is for the relative position of
the deprived and the dominant groups in the two countries, we
can offer a tentative answer to the question asked in a relative
way. We cannot ask whether Harijans are better off in the political
arena than in the economic—that would require comparing votes
with rupees. But we can ask more meaningfully whether the
difference between Harijans and caste-Hindus is greater in one
arena than in another. The comparison still depends on some
tricky problems of comparison across arenas, but it allows one to
come closer to an answer. In the remainder of this chapter we shall
deal with this question from the point of view of measures of
political participation and measures of income and of occupational
and educational levels. In the next chapter, we shall compare the
political and economic arenas from the point of view of some
more directly comparable data—the comparative availability of
careers for deprived groups within the private and the public
sectors.

In Table 37, we present the measures of association between
caste or race and a variety of economic indicators and political
indicators. Because of the difference in the nature of the
measurement for the various items, they are not really
comparable, but the overall pattern is suggestive. In general, the
measures of association are higher for the socioeconomic variables
than for the political—indicating that the deprived and dominant
groups are more like each other in relationship to politics than in
relation to social and economic indicators. Only in relation to
citizen-initiated contacts does the difference between deprived and
dominant group approach the magnitude of the group differences
in the socioeconomic sphere. If the political system is the path to
equality, our data suggest that it is indeed more equalitarian than
the economy.

Table 37

THE RELATIONSHIP OF RACE AND CASTE WITH SOME
SOCIOECONOMIC AND POLITICAL INDICATORS

SocioEconomic Indicators	United States	India	Politicization	United States	India
Education	.26*	.30	Voting	.13	−.03
Family income	.26	.34	Citizen-initiated contacts	.19	.10
Occupational levels	.49	.51	Campaign activities	.10	.04
Material possessions	**	.40	Cooperative activities	.03	.05
Family socio-economic level (overall scale)	.52	.55			
Exposure to mass media of communication	.16	.33			

*Figures are Somers' D.

**Not available.

A more reliable comparison of the degree of equality found in the political and socioeconomic spheres is found in Figures 6 and 7. The reader will remember that in Chapter III we compared the four groups in terms of a general standardized scale of socioeconomic status—based on a combined measure of income, occupational level, educational attainment, and ownership of material possessions. Though there are complex measurement difficulties in connection with such a scale, it provides a fairly good indicator of how much any individual receives or has received of the social and economic benefits of society; and it is even more reliable in answering the question of whether any one individual receives more or less than another. Lastly, the scale has the advantage of allowing standardization. In Chapter III we divided the scale into six equal parts. The division is arbitrary—in that we do not argue that society has six classes—but it is most useful in comparing the ranking of groups. If a group is over- or underrepresented in the upper sixth we know something about its hierarchical position. More important, the division into equal groups opens the possibility of comparing across societies and, relevant for our present concerns, comparing across different hierarchical scales.

In Figures 6A and 6B, we do the latter for the United States. We have built a scale of political participation (see Appendix) based on all the political acts we have measured. The population was then divided into equal sixths depending on the score on this scale. Like the socioeconomic hierarchical scale, this scale provides a fairly reliable indication of how any two individuals rank on participation; and the division into equal intervals allows us to compare this scale with the scale on socioeconomic position. If Blacks are not disadvantaged on participation, they should form the same proportion at each level of the scale of participation; and if they are in the same relative position in relation to participation as they are in relation to socioeconomic status, they should form the same proportion in the top category of the socioeconomic scale as in the participation scale, in the next category, and so forth.

If we consider Figure 6 and look first at the distribution of Blacks and whites on the various levels of the participation scale, we see a clear pattern of deprivation. Blacks are less likely to fall in the highest participation categories than one would expect, given their proportion in the society and more likely to fall in the lower categories. Thus they are about eleven percent of our sample; if they were equally represented in participation, they would represent eleven percent of each level of the participation scale. However, they are ten percent of the top category and nineteen percent of the bottom category.

The distribution in relation to participation, on the other hand, is quite a bit less skewed in favor of whites than is the distribution in relation to socioeconomic benefits. If one compares SES with participation (Figures 6A and 6B), one sees that Blacks are much more underrepresented in the top one-sixth of the socioeconomic scale than in the top one-sixth of the participation scale. Equal representation would have eleven percent of them in the top category; in fact, they form ten percent of the category on the participation scale, and only two percent of that category on the socioeconomic scale. Switching to the bottom of the scale, we find that the lowest sixth of participation contains nineteen percent Blacks while the lowest sixth on socioeconomic benefits contains thirty-six percent Blacks (compared with the eleven percent one would expect in each case). Indicative of the greater disparity between the races on the socioeconomic scale than on the participation scale is the fact that Somers' D measure of association between race and the socioeconomic scale is .52 while the association between race and the participation scale is .07.

If we turn to the data on India, we find a similar pattern. If we consider Figure 7A we see hardly any deprivation for Harijans in relation to the participation rates for caste-Hindus. Harijans are about sixteen percent of our Indian sample (of Hindus only). They are underrepresented in the topmost category of participation, forming only twelve percent of that category. But on the bottom end of the scale, we find that they are also a bit underrepresented. They form only fifteen percent of that category, reflecting the higher rates at which Harijans vote.*

---

*The data would show more skewing of Harijan activity if we had used a participation scale without voting. Harijans would then be slightly over-represented in the lowest category—they form twenty-one percent of the lowest category on a participation scale without voting in comparison with the sixteen percent one expects if they were proportionately represented.

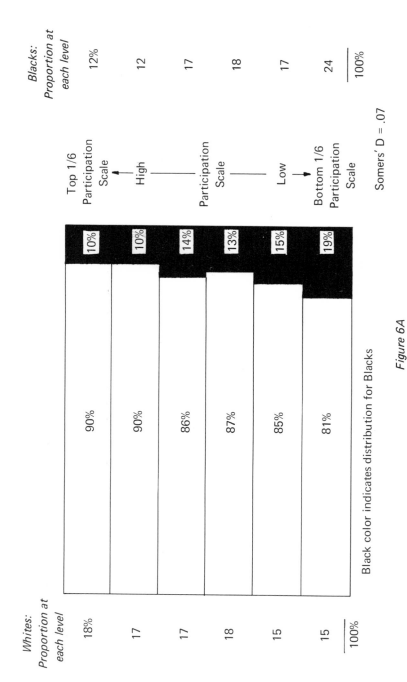

Blacks:
Proportion at
each level

12%

12

17

18

17

24
‾‾‾‾
100%

Top 1/6
Participation
Scale

← High

Participation
Scale

Low →

Bottom 1/6
Participation
Scale

Somers' D = .07

Black color indicates distribution for Blacks

Figure 6A

PARTICIPATION SCALE: PROPORTION WHITE AND BLACK AT EACH LEVEL

Whites:
Proportion at
each level

18%

17

17

18

15

15
‾‾‾‾
100%

10% / 90%

10% / 90%

14% / 86%

13% / 87%

15% / 85%

19% / 81%

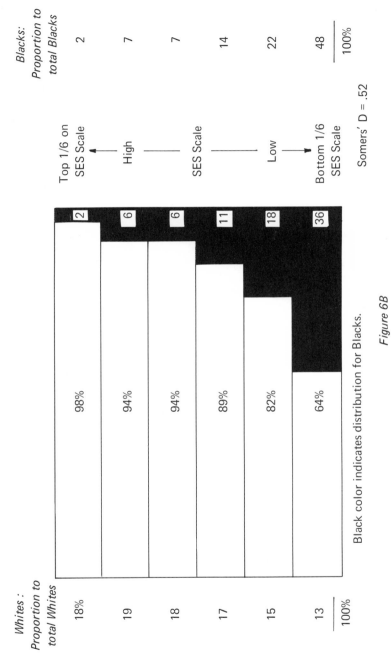

Blacks:
Proportion to
total Blacks

2

7

7

14

22

48
100%

Top 1/6 on SES Scale

High

SES Scale

Low

Bottom 1/6 SES Scale

Somers' D = .52

2

6

6

11

18

36

98%

94%

94%

89%

82%

64%

Whites :
Proportion to
total Whites

18%

19

18

17

15

13
100%

Black color indicates distribution for Blacks.

Figure 6B

FAMILY SOCIOECONOMIC STATUS (SES) OF WHITES AND BLACKS

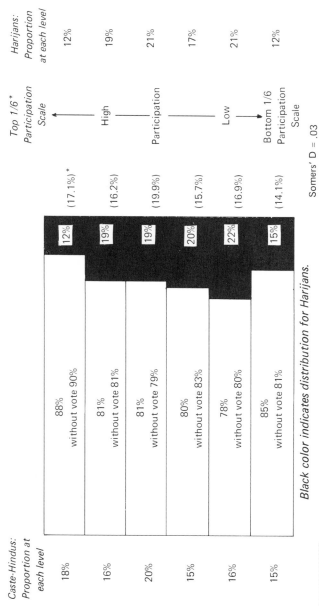

Black color indicates distribution for Harijans.

Somers' D = .03

*The top and bottom categories contain 1/6 of the population as does the second category from the bottom. Some of the other categories are somewhat larger or smaller than one-sixth due to the distribution on the participation scale. This has little effect on the data within the individual horizontal bars. It should be taken into account in considering the figures in the columns on the right and left of the graph—i.e., the proportions of Harijans or Caste-Hindus on each level. The figures in parentheses to the right of the horizontal bars indicate the proportion of the entire sample on each level. This should be compared with the proportion of the dominant and deprived group.

Figure·7A

PARTICIPATION SCALE: PROPORTION CASTE-HINDU AND HARIJAN AT EACH LEVEL (including Voting)

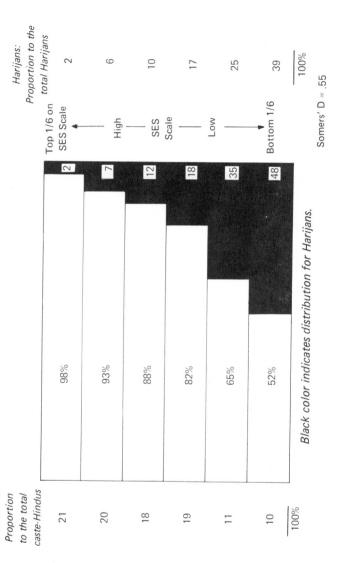

Caste-Hindus:
Proportion
to the total
caste-Hindus

21

20

18

19

11

10

—
100%

Harijans:
Proportion to the
total Harijans

2

6

10

17

25

39

—
100%

Top 1/6 on
SES Scale

High

SES
Scale

Low

Bottom 1/6

Somers' D = .55

98%

93%

88%

82%

65%

52%

2

7

12

18

35

48

Black color indicates distribution for Harijans.

Figure 7B

FAMILY SOCIOECONOMIC STATUS (SES) OF CASTE-HINDUS AND HARIJANS

But, when we compare the data of the participation section of Figure 7 to those of the socioeconomic section, we find a situation parallel to that in the United States. The degree of inequality is much greater in relation to the socioeconomic scale than it is in relation to the political participation scale. In the socioeconomic scale, the Harijans form only two percent of the top category, while at the bottom of the scale, we find them forming forty-eight percent of the most deprived group. Equality would have found them forming sixteen percent of each group. And, as in the United States, the measures of association are much greater between caste and socioeconomic position (Somers' D = .55) than between caste and political participation (Somers' D = .03)*   Indeed, the difference in the measures of association across the two hierarchies is strikingly similar in India and the United States. (Somers' D is .52 and .55 for the United States and India respectively for socioeconomic status and .07 and .03 for political activity for the two countries.)

On the basis of these data, can one say that the political system is more open for deprived groups than is the socioeconomic system? Our answer is yes, but one must be cautious in interpreting the meaning of this. In comparing between the scales of participation and of socioeconomic benefits we are not comparing incomparables insofar as we think of the comparison as one between *similar* positions on *different* hierarchies. When one considers that proportion of the population that receives most of the social and economic benefits of the society, one finds very few Blacks or Harijans. When one considers a similarly sized group that participates most frequently in political life, one finds a higher proportion of Blacks and Harijans than on the socioeconomic scale.

On the other hand, the comparison across the socioeconomic and the political status systems is difficult. The socioeconomic variables along which we array the four groups represent "payoffs": income, possessions, education, a high-status job. The political variables represent access to channels of influence that may eventuate in payoffs but that are, aside from the value of and gratification from taking part per se, not yet payoffs.

---

*Somers' D for Caste and Participation scale without voting would be somewhat higher—.09, but not much.

Yet the comparison clearly suggests that the political system is more open and egalitarian than is the socioeconomic system. We have suggested a number of reasons for this: One is the greater strength of the egalitarian ideology in the political sphere than in the nonpolitical sphere. Another is the greater likelihood that egalitarian ideals will lead to egalitarian reality in the political rather than in the private sector because of the greater "public" nature of the former. In addition, the political potency of a group—in terms of voting strength or ability to protest and embarrass officials—may grow more easily than does their economic or social prowess, and this creates further pressure for the opening of the political system. And, lastly, there may be incumbents of political office—either members of the deprived group or not—who find it expedient to obtain the support of such groups. But, for whatever reasons, the channels of ascent through the political system would seem to exceed those through the socioeconomic system.

One ought not to overinterpret this conclusion. The political system in neither country is egalitarian. Note in particular that the more intense and difficult the activity, the less the equality. And we do not measure activities that represent very high levels of political potency; all our measures are of activities likely to be carried on by a mass public. Yet it is just the more potent and less frequent acts that may lead to the greatest payoff. This last point is crucial, and returns us to a point made above. The relative equality in mass political activity does not necessarily imply relative equality in successful political activity. Suppose Blacks or Harijans always voted and always voted as a cohesive group for particular candidates. There could be no more potent way to take part in voting. But the candidate might always lose. Or he might be elected and ineffective. Or members of a deprived group might contact and contact in large numbers. But that which they contact about is unattainable, or is rejected, or, as the data in Chapter V showed, is likely to be more narrowly defined than that about which whites or caste-Hindus contact. They would therefore participate as much as others, but achieve less.

The point we are making is that participation is not the same as influence. We have considered differences in participation, not the more important differences in successful participation. To deal with the latter, we would need more refined data.

Chapter VIII

THE GOVERNMENTAL CAREER

We have, thus far, looked at political participation by private citizens. But the greater openness of the polity suggests another way in which a change in the stratification system can be accomplished through the political system—through governmental careers. The government is not only a producer of benefits for the citizenry in general, it is also a major employer and, therefore, a direct source of higher income or of higher-status jobs. In this chapter, we shall look at the government career, and the relative extent to which it is open to members of the deprived groups.

We shall also consider governmental careers at various levels, ranging from employment in the lowest sections of the government, to top elected and appointed positions. Of particular interest, of course, are those jobs that go beyond low and menial labor. Government jobs in general represent alternative sources of employment to the private sector, but higher-level occupations represent real ascent in the society. Upper-level jobs, furthermore, have a dual aspect. On the one hand, they represent opportunities per se for advancement beyond low socioeconomic status. Given a large governmental sector and a greater openness to deprived groups for employment within that sector, the governmental career may be a more than marginal means of changing socioeconomic status. In addition, positions within the government represent potential access to greater benefits for the deprived groups as a whole. This, of course, is the main reason for concern with deprived group representation within the legislative system. In this sense, equality of access to legislative positions has a much broader implication for deprived groups than does equality of access to governmental jobs where there is less decision latitude. Yet, in light of our discussion of the importance of citizen-initiated contacts as a means of linking the individual and the government, opportunities for deprived group representation within the bureaucracy may also represent increased access to the government for private citizens from the deprived group. The ascriptive barriers that inhibit effective contacting for Blacks faced with a white bureaucracy or Harijans faced with a caste-Hindu one would be reduced.

For this reason, we shall consider occupations on all these levels as relevant both as measures of direct social ascent and as measures of potential access to the government and its beneficial outputs for those not themselves so employed.

The reasons one might expect to find the political career system more open than the nonpolitical are similar to those suggested in the previous chapter as to why political participatory opportunities might be more open than opportunities within the socioeconomic sphere. The reasons include the greater potency of egalitarian ideals in the political realm, plus the greater likelihood that they will match reality, the political pressures that the deprived groups can bring to bear to open channels, and so forth. In addition, it may be that government provides more opportunities for low- and middle-level clerical jobs which are prestigious and secure, but offer prestige and security largely to those whose other opportunities are severely limited. The governmental career may, therefore, be particularly attractive to deprived groups.

The comparison of the occupational roles held by Blacks and Harijans represents a good example of the complex intertwining of similarity and difference in social context that permeates our analysis. Traditionally, Harijans engaged only in the lowest occupations, especially those that were considered by the clean castes to be polluting. They have been sweepers, tanners of hides, and agricultural laborers. Such involvement in work that others consider unclean both defines and reaffirms their pariah status in society (de Vos and Wagatsuma, 1966). In the United States, there has never been as clear an ideal definition of the expected occupational roles of Blacks. Yet from at least two points of view, there is similarity. Blacks have, in fact, long held the lowest-status occupations in the society; occupations involving low prestige and low income. Data illustrating the parallel situation for the two deprived groups were presented above. Nor is this situation a "natural" concomitant of other social processes—that is, merely the result of lack of education or of family background that makes the attainment of high-status occupation difficult (see Blau and Duncan, 1967). Over and above these forces, one can find patterns of direct discrimination in hiring and promotion that would parallel (though would not fully match) the institutionalized barriers to occupational attainment in India. And the low-status occupations of Blacks were supported by beliefs as to the "ideal" occupation for Blacks. Phrases like "Negro work" to describe unrewarding and hard manual labor (that happily one hears rarely now) or studies of children's stereotypes of occupational groups, indicate that the occupational status of Blacks was well supported by a belief system (again not as well structured as the Indian belief system about Harijans) as to the appropriateness of their low occupational status.

But the difference in the *justification* for the deprived statuses of the two groups in India and in the United States may have important implications for the policies pursued in the two societies to deal with occupational deprivation. In India, as pointed out in the first chapter, the justification of the lowly position of Harijans derives from beliefs as to the appropriateness of a static hierarchical society. In the United States, paradoxically, the justification may derive from a belief in the appropriateness of an open society; a belief that leads one to consider failure to achieve higher status the result of lack of effort rather than of discriminatory social structures.

The difference in the justifications for the deprivation of Blacks and Harijans may have important implications. In particular, it may affect the use of compensatory programs. Such programs as reserved places in universities, in the government, and in the legislature are more fully institutionalized in India (Galanter, 1963). In America such programs are scattered and informal. In part, the difference may derive from the different ideologies. In India it would be difficult for anyone—whether favoring or opposing Harijan advancement—to deny the existence of discriminatory social structures that have held Harijans in lowly positions. Under such circumstances a commitment to change leads more easily to an acceptance of counter-discriminatory structures. In the United States, the belief that social improvement has always been open to those who try makes counter-discriminatory practices easier to oppose.

Thus, in India, the attempt to change the occupational situation of Harijans has been manifested in a constitutional provision of reserved positions for Harijans in government service, ranging from reservation of positions in the bureaucracy, to positions within universities, to seats in legislative bodies from the village Panchayat to the Lok Sabha in New Delhi. These provisions were supposed to exist for a limited period of time, but they allow for continuation of the special treatment as long as severe disparity exists between the deprived and dominant groups (see Galanter, 1963). In the United States, compensatory hiring and recruitment programs exist, but usually of a more informal sort, without clear definition or governmental sanction.

In interpreting the data to follow, these distinctions must be kept in mind. We are comparing occupational recruitment systems that reflect quite different purposefully designed organizational structures. This point will become apparent when we consider some of the data. Let us turn to them.

Tables 38 and 39 present the proportions of Blacks in various occupational categories in the federal service—Table 38 by service

Table 38

BLACK REPRESENTATION IN FEDERAL GOVERNMENT
BUREAUCRACY BY SERVICE GRADE (1966)

Service Grade	Blacks as Percentage of Total in Each Grade
GS 1 through 4	18
GS 5 through 11	5
GS 12 through 18	1
Total all grades	13

SOURCE: Bureau of Labor Statistics, *Current Population Reports,* "Negro Population," 1968.

Table 39

DISTRIBUTION OF BLACKS IN FEDERAL GOVERNMENT
EMPLOYMENT BY OCCUPATIONAL LEVELS (1966)

Occupational Level	Blacks as Percentage of Total in Each Occupation
Laborers	26
Service workers	17
Operatives	18
Craftsmen and foremen	7
Clerical	10
Managers and officials	3
Professional and technical	8

SOURCE: U. S. Bureau of Labor Statistics, *Current Population Reports,* "Social and Economic Conditions of Negroes" (1967).

grade and Table 39 by type of work performed. The service grade data in Table 38 indicates a slight overproportionality in the numbers of Blacks in the federal service: They form thirteen percent of the federal service (in 1966), a somewhat larger proportion than they are of the total population (about eleven percent). As both tables indicate, however, they are disproportionately in the lower occupational and service-grade categories. Few appear in the upper categories. However, the data are not inconsistent with an interpretation of greater openness for careers in the government than in the private sector. Table 39 indicates that ten percent of the clerical-level employees are Black, a figure twice as large as that in our sample study, which has five percent of clerical jobs occupied by Blacks. And the Table 39 indicates that three percent of the governmental employees in managerial and official positions and eight percent of those in professional and technical positions are Black, a figure that compares with the two percent found in our sample for the combination of those two categories. In general, it seems that the opportunities in the higher reaches of the government—though by no means equally allocated between the two races—are more equally allocated than in the private sector. This interpretation is supported by the data in Table 40, which gives the proportions of Blacks in various occupations roughly (but only roughly) comparable to those found in the upper two categories of Table 39. It is probable that the eight percent of the "professional and technical" category that is Black (Table 39) represents a range of professions reaching lower than most of the more specific categories in Table 40. But the difference in the direction of greater Black employment at higher ranks of the government service than in the private sector occupations reported in Table 2 is sharp enough to confirm our general impression of greater openness in the governmental realm.

In Table 41, we have parallel data on employment by Harijans within the Indian government—including, in this case, data over time. No data are available on the proportion of Harijans employed by the government who are in positions specifically reserved for Harijans. But it is quite likely that, particularly in the higher positions, the numbers reflect both the quota set for government employees and the lack of fulfillment of the quota. The first four columns of Table 41 report data on the four classes

Table 40

REPRESENTATION OF BLACKS IN SOME SELECTED
HIGH-LEVEL "PROFESSIONAL" OCCUPATIONS (1960)

"Professional" Occupation	Blacks* as Percentage of Total in Each Profession
Accountants and auditors	0.6
Chemists	2.1
Engineers	0.5
Lawyers and judges	0.9
Physicians and surgeons	2.0

SOURCE: John P. Davis (ed.), *The American Negro Handbook,* Prentice Hall, New Jersey (1966), p. 570.

*Figures for males only.

Table 41

REPRESENTATION OF SCHEDULED CASTES IN THE CENTRAL GOVERNMENT SERVICES BY SERVICE CLASS

Year	Class IV		Class III		Class II		Class I		Indian Administrative Service (IAS)		Indian Police Service (IPS)	
	Harijans n	% of Total Officers	Harijans n	% of Total Officers	Harijans n	% of Total Officers	Harijans n	% of Total Officers	Harijans n	% of Total IAS	Harijans n	% of Total IPS
1954	8,350	13.2	9,950	5.5	65	1.0	10	0.5	17	1.6	7	1.0
1958	200,921	20.8	51,890	6.4	405	2.1	92	0.9	29	2.0	14	1.8
1962	186,674	17.6	79,719	8.0	769	2.6	239	1.3	68	3.5	39	3.6
1966	211,073	18.0	99,017	8.8	974	3.2	361	1.7	128	5.4	72	5.3

SOURCE: Reports of the Commissioner for Scheduled Castes and Tribes. For figures of 1954, see the report for the year 1956-57. The rest of the table was computed from the report for the year 1964-65. Figures in Class IV category for years 1954 and 1958 include sweepers, the traditional calling of the Harijans, while figures for 1962 and 1966 exclude that. The figures do not include Army, police and judiciary departments. Also the reports note that all departments are not included since many did not supply the information.

of the central government service. As with Blacks, there is greater representation in the lower positions. Indeed, if one compares the lowest row on Table 41 with Table 38, an almost identical pattern appears in terms of the proportions of the various levels who are from the deprived groups. The time trend is also interesting. The increase in numbers at all levels reflects a general growth in the size of the governmental service. More important is the change in the proportions of the various grades coming from Harijan background. These proportions go up most strikingly in the upper grades. In Class IV—the lowest employment grade—there appears to be a decline in absolute numbers and in proportions of Harijans between 1958 and 1962. But this is due to a change in the categorization, such that sweepers—a traditional Harijan occupation—are not included in the data. Thus the data for Class IV indicate a general tendency for Harijans in government service to move into nontraditional occupations.

The data in the last two sets of columns are for the elite all-India services, the Indian Administrative Service and the Indian Police Service. In these categories, the proportions of Harijans have risen substantially. Indeed, Harijans form a larger proportion of these elite services than they do of the lower-ranked Class 1 and Class 2 employees. This quite likely reflects a greater emphasis on and a greater enforcement of quotas in the top and most visible classes of government service, the IAS and the IPS.

There are no comparable data on Harijan employment in the private sector. But it is quite likely—given the existence of reserved positions in the government, given the high prestige and greater security of government employment, given the greater opportunity to enforce nondiscrimination in the governmental sphere—that Harijan occupational mobility out of traditional low-status into higher occupations comes very heavily through the governmental service. There is some evidence that upward mobility in the economic and academic spheres is much more limited for Harijans than upward mobility through government (Isaacs, 1964: 90-102). And there is also evidence that government employment exchanges are increasingly used by Harijans, and used heavily for employment in the central and state governments (Commissioner for Scheduled Castes and Scheduled Tribes, n.d. 94-95).

The data on Black and Harijan representation in the state and national legislatures of the two countries are reported in Tables 42 and 43. The data are strikingly different, the Indian data reflecting the reservation of a number of seats for Harijans proportional to their part of the population, while the data from the United States represent the results of more ordinary, competitive electoral processes. Thus the Indian data indicate that Harijans form about 15% of state and national legislatures, and the proportion does not change much in the fifteen years reported in Table 42. In the United States, the proportions are much lower. In the House of Representatives, the number of Blacks went from four in 1962 to nine in 1970 (and from zero to one for Senators), or from .8% to 2% of the total—far below the 11% that Blacks represent of the population as a whole. And in the state legislatures, the underrepresentation of Blacks is similar. Though the number of Blacks and the proportion of Blacks more than tripled between 1962 and 1970, one still finds that only about 2% of the state legislators are Black in 1970. This, in turn, is a higher proportion than one finds in relation to lesser elective jobs. A survey conducted in 1970 reported that Blacks form but .3% of all elected officials in the United States—on the national, state, and local levels (from a survey conducted by the Metropolitan Applied Research Center and the Voter Education Project of the Southern Regional Council, and reported in the *New York Times* for March 31, 1970).

Yet the change over time cannot be ignored. Blacks in state legislatures for instance, numbered 52 in 1962. Within four years, the number had tripled to 148.

The data for Harijans can tell us less about trends over time, because the basic numbers of Harijans in the various legislatures reflect the governmental decision to reserve a proportional number of seats for Harijan candidates. The data on Table 43 also indicate that almost all seats occupied by Harijans are reserved seats; very few Harijans win elections to seats outside the reserved ones. This, of course, ought not to be taken to indicate that, if the reserved seats were abolished, Harijans would win only the handful of unreserved seats they now win. Given that the political parties must each allocate about fifteen percent of their tickets to Harijans for reserved seats, party leaders have been reluctant to

Table 42

BLACK REPRESENTATION IN FEDERAL AND STATE LEGISLATURES

Year	Members Total n	Black Members n	Blacks as % of Total Members
House of Representatives:			
1962	435	4	0.85
1964	435	5	1.1
1966	435	6	1.3
1970	435	9	2.0
State Legislatures:			
1962	7,638*	52	0.7
1964	7,638	94	1.2
1966	7,638	148	1.9
1970	7,638	168	2.1

SOURCE: Bureau of Labor Statistics, *Current Population Reports,* "Social and Economic Conditions of Negroes in United States," (1967). 1970 data from a survey conducted by the Metropolitan Applied Research Center Inc. and the Voter Education Project of the Southern Regional Council, reported in the *New York Times,* Mar. 31, 1970, p. 1.

*Number based on 1969 figures. May be different in each year but would have little effect on results.

Table 43

HARIJAN REPRESENTATION IN CENTRAL
AND STATE LEGISLATURES

| Year | Members Total n | Harijan Members | | | Harijans as Percentage to Total Members |
		Total	Reserved	Non-Reserved	
Lok Sabha (Parliament):					
1952	489	76	72	4	15.5
1957	494	82	76	6	16.5
1962	494	77	76	1	15.5
1967	520	77	77	—**	14.8
*State Legislatures**					
1952	3,283	487	477	10	14.8
1957	2,906	478	470	8	16.4
1962	3,121	483	471	12	15.4
1967	3,563	503	503	—**	14.1

SOURCE: For voter and reserved seats Reports of Election Commission. For nonreserved seats, Reports of the Commissioner for scheduled Castes and Tribes.

*Figures only for lower houses of states. Figures for Harijans are incomplete as they are not available for all states.

**Not ascertained.

allocate additional unreserved tickets to Harijan candidates. If there were no reserved seats, the number of unreserved seats won might go up substantially. But the reserved seat situation indicates one way in which such institutions come to perpetuate themselves. The reports of the Commissioner for Scheduled Castes and Scheduled Tribes have urged the parties to give unreserved tickets to Harijans, but the parties have been reluctant to do so, given the commitments to reserved seats. Thus the system persists.

One indicator of increasing political awareness of the Harijans is the fact that the reserved seats are contested; and over time, the number of candidates for such seats has increased. In 1962, there were 3.6 Harijan candidates for each reserved seat in the Lok Sabha. In 1967, the number of candidates per seat had risen to 4.4. For the state legislatures, the pattern was the same, though the change was more modest—from 4.3 per seat in 1962 to 4.6 per seat (from the reports of the Election Commission in 1962 and 1967).

The implication of the reserved seats is uncertain—as is the implication of the low number of Blacks in American legislatures. One assumes that the greater the representation of a particular group, the stronger its voice in legislative bodies, and this is probably true. In this sense, though the winning of reserved seats does not accurately reflect the political prowess of a group, the seats are indeed won and occupied by representatives of the deprived groups. And these seats can lead to higher positions. In the central government in New Delhi, Harijans are also well represented in higher levels. They held, in 1964, seven out of forty ministerial posts (eighteen percent).

The data on political careers parallel those on political activities. Of the various sectors of the society, the political system seems more open to deprived group members than the economic system. Again, one must stress that the outcome of all this is uncertain. Though the deprived groups seem to receive a better proportional representation in government than in the private sector, they are still underrepresented—except in cases such as the Indian reserved legislative seats, where they are assured proportionality. And representation in the bureaucracy or the legislature does not imply success in affecting policy or in allocating larger shares of the governmental pie to one's own group. Such is the ordinary expectation, but the potential payoffs from representation are not the natural and inevitable product of representation.

Chapter IX

THE PATHS TO POLITICS

Studies of political mobilization usually focus on the results of
that mobilization.

One finds some more active in politics than others and, if the
more active are found in more "developed" places—in higher
income countries or regions—one assumes that the active
individuals were impelled to participate in some way by their
enhanced social and economic situation. This has been confirmed
numerous times.

Our own research, as well as that of many others, indicates that
social status characteristics such as education, income, occupation,
and the like are closely related to participation rates. But we
would like to go further in the exploration of this process of

political mobilization. For one thing, we have stressed that political activity is not all of a piece; different acts are pursued by different types of people with different consequences. Thus, a voter is not the same as a campaign activist or as an individual who engages in cooperative group activity or as an individual who contacts a government official on some problem. Nor does he differ simply in the degree of his activity—the campaign activist or the cooperative activist is not merely a *more active* voter—he is different in important other respects.* Thus, in asking who is mobilized, we ought not give an answer until we have clarified the question, "Mobilized in what respect?"

But we can go one step further. Political mobilization is, as the term implies, a process and not a result. It is not merely that there are different ways in which individuals can be politically active; there are different ways they can *become* politically active. Not only may the voter differ from the cooperative activist, but two voters may differ substantially if they came to the vote through different processes. The "good citizen" who votes for a particular candidate because he decides on the basis of careful consideration and adequate information that the candidate will maximize the chances of obtaining the governmental performance the voter prefers is quite different from the voter who is "taken" to the polls by others who instruct him on how to vote, and different from the voter who votes out of habit. The mobilized citizen may have been mobilized in a variety of ways, and the way in which he is mobilized may be as important as the fact of his mobilization.**

In the previous sections of this monograph, we have provided data that suggest that, indeed, the same act may mean different things to different individuals. For some, it is accompanied by information and involvement; for others, it is not. It is now appropriate to try to tie together the various earlier sections into a more multivariate analysis. Our major concern is with the paths to

*For an extended discussion of these differences, see Verba and Nie (forthcoming: chs. 3-6).

**For a perceptive discussion of alternative models of mobilization, see Rudolph and Rudolph (1967). They deal with three—vertical, horizontal, and differential—which are similar to those we discuss below, though different largely in terms of some of the key variables that make up the models.

political participation and how these paths differ for different groups and in relation to different acts. We shall be dealing with four different groups—the dominant and deprived group in each country—four different political acts, and five different political orientations. These distinctions are all familiar from earlier sections. But since we want to tie them together, it may be useful to protect the sanity of the reader by indicating step by step what we intend to do.

Our basic model is simple and derives from the political mobilization literature. Changes in social status—higher-status jobs, increased education, higher income—lead (through the intervening processes of media exposure, which we shall not deal with at this time) to mental states (efficacy, empathy, involvement, and the like) that in turn lead to participation.

Status ⟶ New orientations ⟶ Participation

As an example, individuals with more education develop a greater involvement and concern with general social issues and, therefore, participate.

The model is only a beginning. It is only a hypothetical construct against which we can display actual data. The actual set of relationships may differ for different acts or for different groups. For one thing, the significant intervening orientations may differ from act to act or group to group; social status may not play as key a role. In chapter I, we suggested some alternative path models to participation that depended upon which orientation was important in relation to the political act and what role was played by social status. The political orientations that might play alternative intervening roles are five in number and are familiar from earlier, more descriptive discussions:

GENERAL POLITICAL INVOLVEMENT

Here we are dealing with the extent to which the individual is interested in the political life of his community or society; that is, his subjective involvement in matters beyond his own narrow concerns. It is indexed by questions on level of political interest and frequency of political discussion.

POLITICAL KNOWLEDGE

How well-informed is the individual about what is going on within his country or community?

THE PERSONAL RELEVANCE OF GOVERNMENT

Here we are concerned with the extent to which the individual thinks of the government as a relevant problem-solving agency for his most salient personal problems. It is indexed by answers to open questions on the individual's most important personal and family problems, which were followed up by open questions on the group or agency or person whom the respondent believed could provide aid for him in solving the problem. If the government was mentioned as the relevant agency in relation to these problems, we considered the individual to be aware of the personal relevance of government—though this in itself tells us little about the extent to which he is a generally involved political actor.

GROUP CONSCIOUSNESS

Here we are concerned with the extent to which individuals find some group membership salient to themselves. For our particular purposes, the relevant measure is the frequency with which reference is made to race or caste status in answer to a series of open questions about conflicts in the community, dominant groups, and major problems.*

---

*The measure of group consciousness may be somewhat biased toward the consciousness of Blacks rather than that of whites. In the United States, the measure is the frequency of reference to race as a problem or to race as a relevant social category. But while racial identification is probably the proper focus for group consciousness for Blacks, "white" as a status is obviously less salient. Perhaps if the questionnaire were designed better to tap white identifications with particular ethnic groups or other identifications, we would have a stronger measure of white identity. The same is probably not true of Harijans and caste-Hindus. Caste-Hindus would be "group conscious"

PARTISAN IDENTIFICATION

Here we deal with the extent to which the individual is subjectively attached to a political party. Since parties represent a major recruiting mechanism, as well as an anchor point for the political beliefs of individuals, the role of such identifications may be crucial in the path to participation.

These five characteristics are placed in relation to status and activity in Figure 8.*

The difference among the five subjective orientations is most relevant here because they represent alternative ways in which individuals can come to relate to the government. "General political involvement" and perhaps "political information" represent characteristics that are usually associated with political

---

if they identified with their own caste, which is a more meaningful entity than "white race."

Yet we do not believe that group consciousness is applicable only to the Blacks. The fact that "whiteness" is less salient to whites than is blackness to Blacks is not so much a methodological problem as a substantive fact that goes to the heart of what that measure is attempting to measure. The references to blackness, whiteness, or race derive from open questions as to problems facing the individual or community or the bases of social conflict. Reference to other identifications, such as ethnic groups, were possible for whites. Thus, if there were references to other bases of group identification among whites—conflicts among religions, or ethnic groups, or problems having to do with these statuses—we would find them. But such appear most infrequently in our sample. Less than one percent of white respondents would have been added to the group consciousness category if we had accepted mention of ethnic groups as a criterion for group consciousness. In short, the group consciousness measure is in some sense more applicable to Blacks than to whites, but that is more because the former are in fact more conscious of racial identity. In any case, this particular variable is most interesting for comparisons between Blacks and Harijans, and not between Blacks and whites.

*The model can be, of course, much more complicated. In subsequent works we shall consider the intervening role of mass media; organization membership and travel; as well as the effect of the community with which one lives.

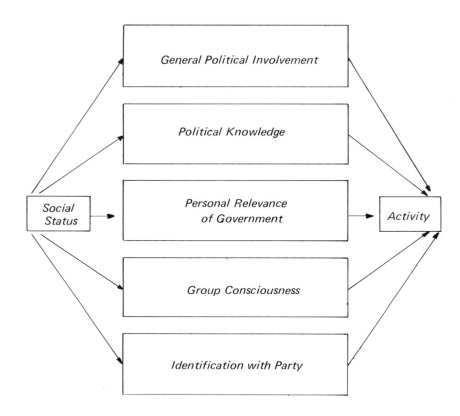

Figure 8
ORIENTATIONS THAT LEAD TO ACTIVITY

activity. They represent measures of a general level of political concern and awareness, concern with societal and communal decisions over and above the personal problems of the individual. They are part of a "civic" syndrome, and are central to most works on participant citizenship. Awareness of the "personal relevance of government" is a kind of political orientation that does not imply concern for problems beyond the specific personal ones of the individual, but does imply awareness of government as related to one's own life. This indexes political involvement, but of a narrow sort. "Group consciousness" implies an awareness of political matters, but largely in relation to the specific position of one's own membership group. It is a differential type of involvement that varies among social groups and does not vary simply with social status. And "partisan attachment" represents a mode of involvement in politics through connection to a political party; a mode of attachment that can be more passive.

Using these five orientations and the relationship, on the one hand, to social status (which we shall index by education level) and, on the other hand, to activity, we can suggest four different models of mobilization.

In Figure 9 we present diagramatic representations of these four mobilizational models. We have placed thick arrows to signify where we expect to find a significant path; we have placed dotted arrows where we expect to find no path; and we have placed thin arrows where our expectations are not clear or where we expect a weak relationship. Thus, in comparing the four models, the solid paths and the dotted paths are most important.

The "Normal" Socioeconomic Model

This is, in a sense, the standard model that has been hypothesized about the relation of participation to development. Individuals with higher statuses (more education, and so on) develop a greater general orientation to politics (they become more involved in and concerned with political matters; they get more information; they have a set of civic norms that fosters participation). And this in turn leads to participation. The important characteristics of this model are the paths running from social status through general political involvement and knowledge,

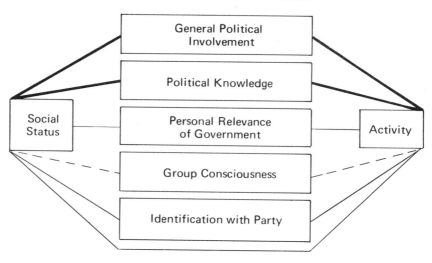

A — Normal Socioeconomic Model

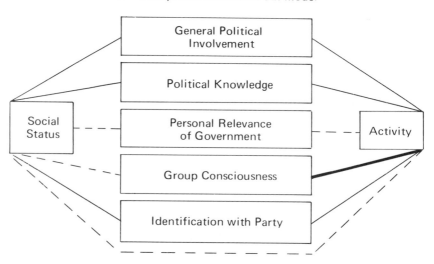

B — Group Consciousness Path Model

Figure 9

SOME HYPOTHETICAL PATHS TO PARTICIPATION

C — Parochial Participation Path Model

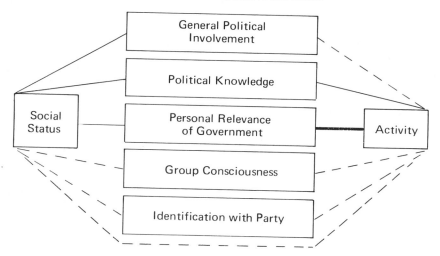

D — Partisan Mobilized Path Model

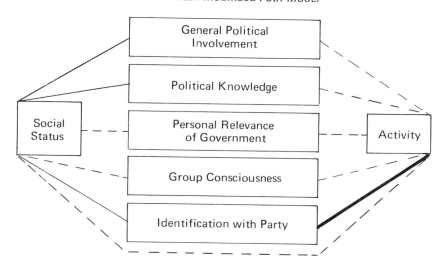

Figure 9 (continued)

SOME HYPOTHETICAL PATHS TO PARTICIPATION

and in turn to political activity. In addition, an important path runs directly from status to participation.

This model is the one that, with variations, has been confirmed in the data on political mobilization when models of this sort are applied to national populations. As mentioned in the first section, it is a model which, if it operates, can hurt the interests of deprived groups, largely because of the crucial role played by socioeconomie status. If the socioeconomic model operates, those who already have the most that the society has to offer (the most education, income, and so on) will participate most.

The Group Consciousness Model

This is the path to participation of self-conscious social groups who share a sense of deprivation. The key variable is the extent of group consciousness. The "personal relevance of government" should play no role, since the group-conscious individual is thinking beyond his personal problems; but general involvement, partisanship, and information might play a role. Social status, so important in the "normal" model, should be less relevant. Self-consciousness of one's deprived status replaces that. Social status may, however, play some role in relation to the development of information.

The "Parochial" Model of Participation

This model differs from the "standard" model in that general political involvement plays little role. Rather, the specific contingent problems that the individual has and the perceived "personal relevance of government" are important. Information about the government may still be relevant, and that may in turn be affected by social status. But the key characteristic of this set of paths is the absence of a role played by political orientations beyond those very narrow ones associated with the individual's own problems—there is no path from general political involvement, nor from group consciousness, nor from partisanship.

The "Partisan Mobilized" Model

This model resembles the group consciousness model in several respects; in particular, in the relatively weak role of social status. But the distinguishing characteristic of this model is the absence of paths to participation that derive from an individual's sense of the relevance of politics to him—general involvement, group consciousness, or personal relevance of government. Rather, attachment to a party plays a major role. Those for whom this forms the path to participation are most likely individuals who are externally mobilized—that is, their political participation does not derive from an internalized set of expectations about government or an involvement in political matters.

In Figure 9 we assume a causal ordering such that education (the social status measure we use in these examples) may affect political orientations, but not vice versa. In turn, the orientations may affect political activity, but not vice versa. We do not specify an order among the orientations.

The absence of an expected causal ordering among the orientations is, at this time, justified for two reasons: for one thing, such orderings should be made on the basis of considerations such as time-order or pliability, and we have no clear expectations with regard to these. More important, we feel that for the type of analysis we are doing, the ordering among the five types of orientation may not be important. We are not looking for the single best-fitting path to participation. If we were, the absence of an ordering among the orientations would greatly reduce the interest of the findings. We are, rather, looking for differences in importance among these orientations as one considers alternative groups or alternative acts.

We can now fit our data to diagrams similar to those in Figure 9. The question is: What do the paths to participation look like for the different groups and, for each group, for the different modes of participation? For what group and for what act do we find approximations of the normal socioeconomic model; for which groups do we find approximations of other models? Or do the data not fit any of these models?

Several comments ought to be made about how we are treating the data that go into the models. The first has to do with the way in which we treat caste and race. If one is interested in the relationship between caste or race and political mobilization, and one is using, as we are using, a form of statistical causal modelling, one can handle race or caste in one of two ways. Race or caste as "variables" (as ordinal rankings) can be entered into the model and one can see how important they are as a "causes" of participation. In that case, one would have a causal model that looked something like the following:

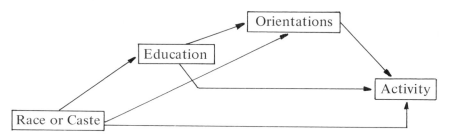

We would assume that race or caste were the first variables in the causal chain, and see how they affect activity—whether their impact is direct or through education and political attitudes.

Our approach is different. We develop a causal model using other characteristics (in this case, education and the five orientations) and see how that model "works" when applied to the different racial and the different caste groups. This latter approach tells one less about how important race or caste is in leading to political activity (we have tried to do that in earlier sections of this book), but a lot more about how the social and psychological *processes* that lead to participation work *within* these groups. Our assumption is, thus, that these are different populations within which social processes may operate differently. From a statistical point of view, this latter approach does not require an assumption of the absence of interaction between caste and race and the other variables. Indeed, our assumption is that there is interaction—that orientation and education relate differently to each other and to participation within the several groups.

A second point has to do with our inability to place the various orientations in a causal order. This raises the problem of how to relate the various orientations to the dependent variables. If one relates each orientation to the activity measure that is the dependent variable, controlling only for the prior impact of education, one is ignoring the effect on that particular orientation of the other orientations; and one does not have a full path model containing education and all the orientations. On the other hand, if one relates each orientation to the activity measure, controlling for education and the prior impact of all other orientations, one may be controlling too much, since from each orientation one will have removed the effect of all the others. And given a moderately strong relationship among some of them, there may be little relationship left.

Our compromise is to present both measures: controlling for education, and for education and the orientations. The relevant data are in Figures 10, 11, 12 and 13. Each figure contains data for one of the groups we are studying: whites, Blacks, caste-Hindus, or Harijans. And on each figure there is a path model relevant to each of the four types of activity. The reader must accept our apologies for sixteen diagrams of this sort, but the differences across groups and across acts are, we believe, interesting enough to warrant such consideration.

The figures on the following diagrams are:

(a) *The coefficients on the paths from education to the orientations.* These represent the simple correlations between education and the orientations, and they also represent the path coefficients from education to the orientations. (That is, if a pair of individuals differs in their level of education by one standard unit, the expected difference in the orientational variable for this same pair is given by this number.)

(b) *The numbers without parentheses on the paths from the orientational variables to the activity measure.* These indicate the degree of contribution of orientations to participation, independent of education. They are path coefficients in the three-variable causal system:

(This means that if two persons have the same degree of education but differ on the attitude by one standard unit, their expected difference on participation will be given by this number.)

(c) *The figure in parentheses on the path from the orientations to activity.* This represents the degree of contribution of the orientation to the activity independent of education and the other four orientational variables. It represents the path coefficients in the seven-variable causal model:

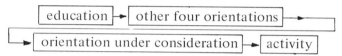

(This means that if two individuals have the same education and are the same on all the other attitudes, but differ by one standard unit on the attitude under consideration, they will differ by one standard unit on the activity.)

(d) *The figure on the path from education directly to the activity.* This is the direct effect of education on the activity, controlling for all five orientations. (If we had a pair of persons who had exactly the same values on all five orientations but they differed by one standard unit in education, the figure represents the expected difference in activity.)

The reader—to whom we again apologize—can read these figures in several ways. We recommend the first way (A) listed below, but some may prefer to consider the diagrams in ways B and C as well.

(A) If one considers the figures outside of parentheses—the coefficients on the paths from education to the orientations, from the orientations to the activity, and from education to the activity—one has a good indication of the relative importance of education for the various orientations, of the importance of the orientations for the particular activity (controlling for education), and of the impact of education after one has controlled for the attitudes. This can be interpreted as a series of five three-variable path models:

This way of looking at the data does not really involve a full path model across all seven variables, but for our purposes of comparing the changes in the importance of various orientations as one moves from act to act and from group to group, the data are probably most meaningful in this form.

(B) If one wanted a fuller path model, one would consider the figures in parentheses on the paths from the orientations to the activities. These are the true path coefficients in the seven-variable model and indicate the impacts of the orientations controlling in each case for all other orientations.

(C) The reader familiar with path analysis would still be missing something if he wanted a full path model. These are the paths among the orientations (ten paths in all). These have not been entered (but will be sent to the reader who wants to draw the full diagram).

Lastly, we can note that the substantive result from looking at the diagrams from the points of view of A, B, or C is the same. Thus we recommend looking at the figures—as we shall—outside the parentheses.

Relatively strong paths (over .25) are indicated by heavy solid lines; moderate paths (between .1 and .25) by thinner lines; and the absence of a positive path (under .1) by a dotted line.

Consider first Figure 10 containing data on white Americans. In general, the data for all four activities fit the normal socioeconomic model of mobilization fairly well. Education is closely related to activity. In addition, with the exception of voting, there is a direct impact of education on activity—i.e., after one has controlled for the orientations, there is still a relationship between education and activity. The "personal relevance of government" apparently plays little role in relation to any of the activities, nor does group consciousness. And partisan identification plays a role—as one might expect—in relation to voting and campaign activity, though not in relation to cooperative and contact activity.

The data on white Americans forms a good base line against which to consider the data on the other groups. It fits the normal model fairly well. Higher status brings with it general political involvement and, in turn, that leads to activity.

The data on Figure 11 for Blacks provide some parallels and some striking contrasts. The path to campaign activity for Blacks (Figure 11B) provides us with a good approximation of the group consciousness path to participation. Two features are important

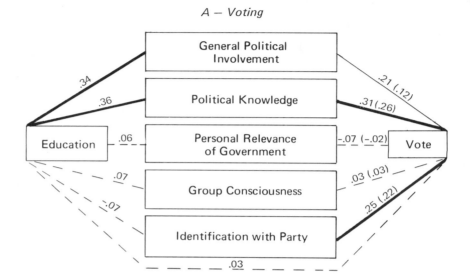

A — Voting

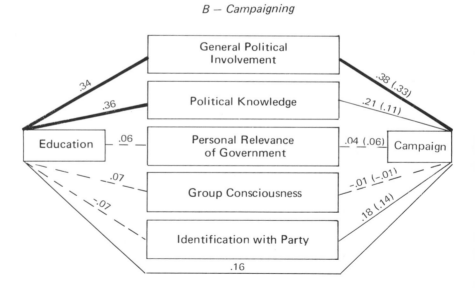

B — Campaigning

Figure 10

PATHS TO PARTICIPATION FOR WHITE AMERICANS

C — Cooperative Activity

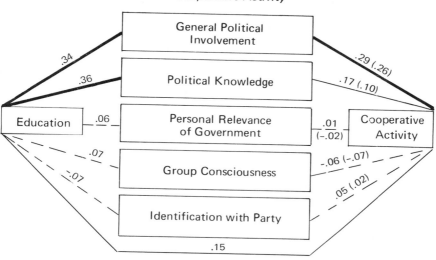

D — Contacting

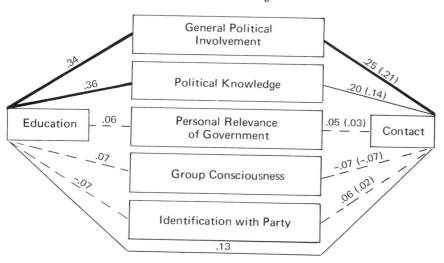

Figure 10 (continued)

PATHS TO PARTICIPATION FOR WHITE AMERICANS

A — Voting

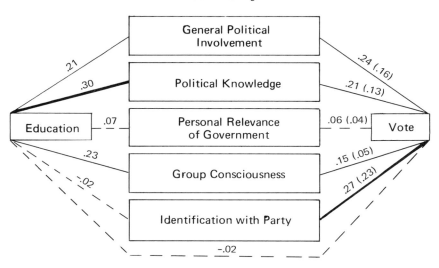

B — Campaigning

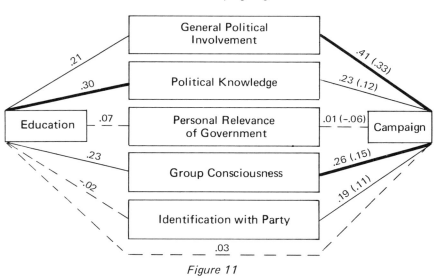

Figure 11

PATHS TO PARTICIPATION FOR BLACK AMERICANS

C — Cooperative Activity

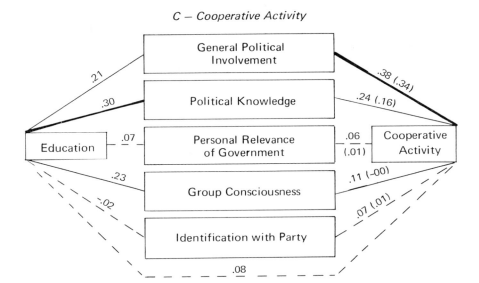

D — Contacting

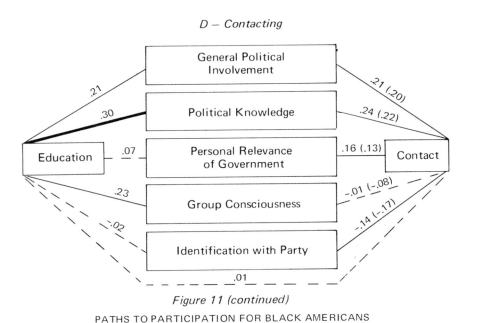

Figure 11 (continued)
PATHS TO PARTICIPATION FOR BLACK AMERICANS

about that path: the important role played by group consciousness and the absence of a direct path from education to activity. This contrasts with the path to campaign activity for whites where group consciousness (as one might expect) played no role. It also contrasts with the path for whites in that education played an important role whereas it plays little or none in relation to Black campaign activity (as is not so clearly expectable). Other orientational variables are also important in relation to Black campaign activity. Interest, information, partisan identification, and, to a lesser extent, personal relevance of government play a role.

Compare the path to campaign activity with the paths to the other activities for Blacks. Voting is similar to campaign activity (Figure 11A), except that it is more weakly related to involvement and group consciousness, though they both play a role. The path is similar to that for whites, with the exception of the stronger role of personal relevance of government and group consciousness.

Figure 11D—the figure for contacting activity for Blacks—is in clear contrast to Figure 11B for campaign activity. The latter approximates the group consciousness model because of the important role of that variable. The former approximates the parochial path to participation better because of the important role of the personal relevance of government. Whereas the path from group consciousness to campaign activity was strong for Blacks (.26) and that from personal relevance nonexistent (.01), the situation is reversed in terms of contacts. The path from group consciousness to contacts is .01 while that from personal relevance is .16. And whereas partisan identification was positively related to campaign activity, it is negatively related to contacting. (The contrast among different acts for the same population is, incidentally, methodologically very useful and quite convincing as to the "reality" of the differences in importance among these various orientations. That they play so different a role for different activities for the same group—where problems of accuracy of measurement of the variable, differences in distribution of the variable, and so on are kept constant—is good evidence that the distinctions are substantive ones in the data and not measurement artifacts.)

The data suggest that campaigning and contacting for American Blacks are quite different modes of activity; the former represents a group based activity relevant to strategies of group advance, the latter represents a much more individualistic activity oriented to the obtaining of specific benefits for the individual and his family. The Black who engages in campaign activity is mobilized, at least in part by his sense of group membership and only slightly by particularistic salient needs. In contrast, the "path" to a contact with the government tends to be more particularistic, based upon perception of the specific relevance of the government to the individual.

Lastly we can consider cooperative activity by Blacks (Figure 11C). It apparently shares some of the characteristics of various activities. Partisan identification plays no role, whereas the more general political orientations—involvement and information—are important. Both personal relevance and group consciousness play a role, but the former plays a bigger one. It would be hard to assign the figure to one of our four hypothetical models. It suggests that there is a variety of forces—particularistic concern with problems and general concern with the group—acting on this kind of activity.

Figure 12 contains the data on the paths to the four acts for caste-Hindus. The paths to cooperative activity and contacting (Figures 12C and 12D) represent fairly good approximations of the normal socioeconomic path to participation. Education leads to general political involvement and information, and these, in turn, lead to activity. Consistent with that model, education itself has a direct effect on activity when the intervening effect of these orientations is partialled out. However—and here the contrast with the data for both whites and Blacks in the United States is interesting—partisan identification plays a role in connection with these two non-electoral activities. This is not, in itself, inconsistent with the expectations of the "normal" model. It does suggest a more pervasive role for partisanship in Indian politics than in American politics; in the United States, cooperative activity and contacting appear to be relatively nonpartisan. The path from partisanship to cooperative activity for whites is .05 and from partisanship to contact is .06; for Blacks the parallel figures are .07 and −.14. For caste-Hindus the respective paths are .20 and .18.

A – Voting

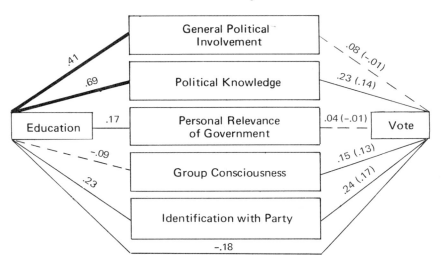

B – Campaigning

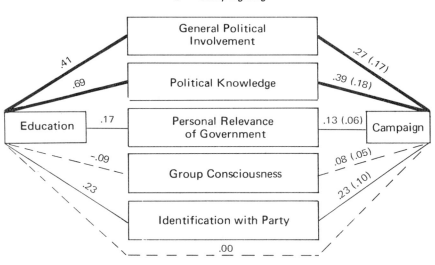

Figure 12

PATHS TO PARTICIPATION FOR CASTE-HINDUS

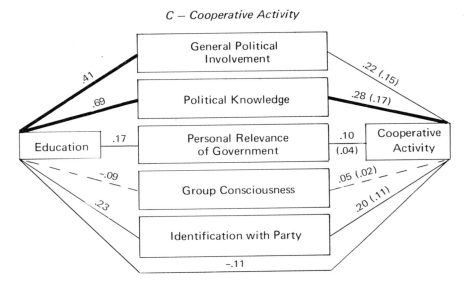

C – Cooperative Activity

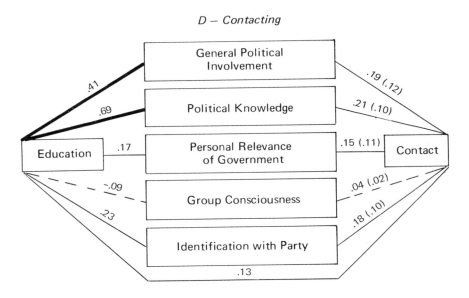

D – Contacting

Figure 12 (continued)

PATHS TO PARTICIPATION FOR CASTE-HINDUS

The two activities in the electoral realm—campaigning and voting—are characterized by the fact that education has no direct impact. Indeed for voting, the direct impact is negative (−.18 when one has partialled out attitudes). For caste-Hindu voting, group consciousness plays a role (the only activity for which it does and the only example of a positive role for group consciousness among members of the dominant group in either society) suggesting an important place in India for voting on the basis of caste affiliation. Political involvement plays no role in relation to the vote, but political information does. It is hard to characterize caste-Hindu voting unambiguously in terms of our four models. In part, it resembles the normal model; education leads to information and, in turn, it leads to activity, but the absence of relationship between general political involvement and the vote, as well as the negative direct relationship between education and the vote, suggests that this model is not appropriate. The combination of group consciousness and partisanship suggest that one may have a path to voting that (weakly) approximates a cross between the partisan mobilized model and the group consciousness model; a mobilization by party on the basis of caste affiliation, perhaps.

Campaign activity, on the other hand, is a good approximation of the normal model, with information, partisan identification and involvement playing major intervening roles between education and activity. Education plays no direct role once the intervening effects of attitudes are partialled out, but the role of education through attitudes is strong.

In short, caste-Hindus may be said to approximate the normal socioeconomic status model, but with interesting qualifications: in particular, the vote does not fit the model well because of the absence of a positive path from general political involvement to activity to voting. And for electoral activities—voting and campaigning—education acts only through political orientations rather than independently as well.

Lastly we turn to Figure 13 and the data on Harijans. Harijan voting is the most distinctive activity. The path to voting for Harijans is a close match to the partisan mobilized model. What is striking is the total absence of relationship between the vote and any political orientation except partisan identification. Neither general political involvement, nor knowledge, nor group consciousness nor awareness of the personal relevance of government is related to the vote. And education per se has a somewhat negative effect on voting. The evidence clearly points to a path to participation that does not derive from an internalized concern with politics—neither as a general concern with community nor societal affairs, nor a manifestation of group awareness, nor even a concern with the particularistic relevance of the government.

The other three activities are in sharp contrast. Cooperative activity and contacting are quite close approximations of the normal socioeconomic model—the major paths run from education through general involvement and information to activity. In addition, education has a quite strong direct effect on activity when one has controlled for orientations. And, as with caste-Hindus (and in contrast with both American groups) partisan identification also plays a role in relation to cooperative and contacting activity.

Campaign activity is similar to cooperative activity and contacting, with the exception that group consciousness is also an important component in the path leading to this kind of activity. In this the contrast with voting is striking. Self-conscious awareness of group membership as a relevant political phenomenon leads to campaign activity, but not to voting.

In understanding the contrast between voting and the other three activities for Harijans, it is well to keep in mind the fact that Harijans vote very frequently: they are as likely to be regular voters as are caste-Hindus and, indeed, as are white or Black Americans. The numbers of Harijans who are active beyond the vote is small. It is small in comparison to the numbers of caste-Hindus who are active in these other ways, and it is small in comparison to the numbers of Harijans who vote.

What we are observing are two different processes operating in relation to political mobilization. A large proportion of the Harijans are mobilized to vote, but the mobilization is external. It has little to do with their involvement in politics or their group consciousness. A smaller group is mobilized into campaign activity, cooperative activity, and contacting. For them, the process of mobilization seems to involve more internalized

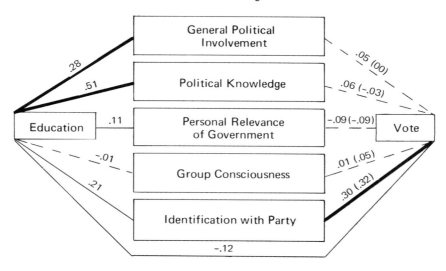

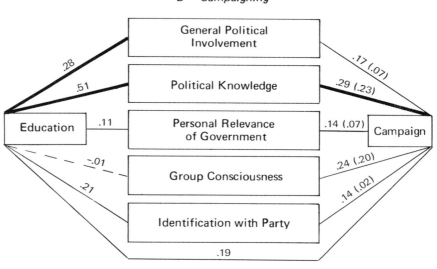

Figure 13

PATHS TO PARTICIPATION FOR HARIJANS

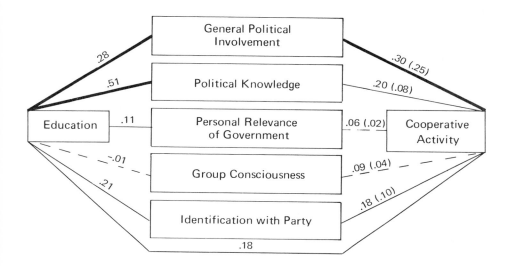

C — Cooperative Activity

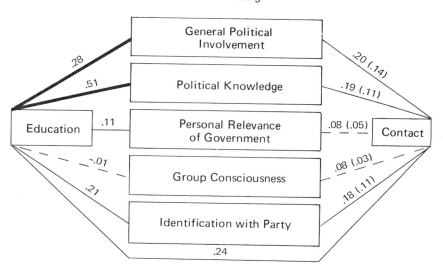

D — Contacting

Figure 13 (continued)

PATHS TO PARTICIPATION FOR HARIJANS

politicization. The campaign activists among Harijans seem to come to their activity through the same path as do Black Americans (compare Figure 13B with Figure 11B); in particular, the role of group consciousness is similar. And, in relation to cooperative and contacting activity, the paths to participation are quite close to the normal socioeconomic model. The contrasting role of education in relation to voting and the other three activities is instructive here. The Harijan voter is actually likely to be somewhat lower in education; for other activities, education plays a powerful positive role even when the intervening effects of orientations are partialled out.

The data represent a good example of the way in which different paths to participation can operate for different activities. The path by which a large number of Harijans come to vote is quite different from the path by which a much smaller number of Harijans come to participate in politics beyond the vote. In the former case, they are mobilized from outside (outside the individual, not necessarily outside the Harijan group); in the latter, their own internal involvement in politics plays a role.

The data are, we believe consistent with our hypotheses as to the impact on Harijan political activity of their absolutely low level of educational attainment and the dispersed character of the group. It would be difficult, we suggested, for the group to develop a sense of identity that would impell it toward political activity and, to some extent, to overcome the handicap of low status. What the data indicate is that this is true in relation to the bulk of Harijans. Where there is mass Harijan participation, one finds that participation dominated by partisan mobilization with no impact of group consciousness. But where there is a more active type of participation in campaigns and where a much thinner slice of Harijans take part, group consciousness takes over.

SUMMATION

We can sum up these findings by the following conclusions:

(1) *For white Americans,* the normal socioeconomic model holds fairly well. Education leads to general political involvement, and that, in turn, leads to political activity.

(2) *For Blacks,* the model does not hold well. A group mobilization model—dominated by a positive role for group consciousness and no role for social status—is a good fit to the data on campaign activity, and a fair approximation to the data on voting and cooperative activity. For contacting, we find that group consciousness plays no role; this is a much more particularistic and much less political (in a broad sense of the term) activity.

(3) *For caste-Hindus* the normal socioeconomic model is a good approximation for cooperative and contacting activity. For voting, one has perhaps a bit of the normal socioeconomic model plus some partisan mobilization along caste lines. And in relation to campaign activity, one has the same with a stronger role for group consciousness. Clearly multiple processes are at work.

(4) *For Harijans,* the partisan mobilized model is a good fit for voting, the group consciousness model for campaign activity, and the normal socioeconomic model for cooperative and contacting activity. The different sizes of the activist groups for these different activities suggest that different processes take place for most Harijans and for the small segment of Harijans who are active beyond the vote.

(5) *Lastly,* one ought to comment on the greater role played by party identification in India. In the United States, cooperative and contacting activities seem to be nonpartisan—at least, party identification plays no role in leading to these activities. In India, party identification is an important factor in both types of activity for both groups.

Chapter X

GROUP CONSCIOUSNESS
AND THE FUTURE

We have in this volume spelled out four models of political mobilization. The first, the "normal socioeconomic model," is one by which those of higher social status develop a series of civic attitudes that lead them to participate. If members of deprived groups who are low in socioeconomic status are to participate enough in politics to redress this situation, one of the other mdoels must operate. Each of these alternative models depends on a key attitudinal component: the external mobilization model in the particular partisan form it takes in our analysis depends on allegiance to a political party and involves participation in the absence of other forms of internal motivation; the group consciousness model depends on a sense of group belonging, and the parochial participation model depends on an awareness of the relevance of government action to the narrow particularized problems of the individuals.

And we have found instances of these alternative forces at work as we have considered the various types of activity engaged in by Blacks and Harijans. But of the three ways in which the "normal socioeconomic model" can be bypassed, the group consciousness way is probably the most crucial for deprived groups. Citizens can come to participate through the "parochial" path of awareness of government for their own particularistic problems. But, as we have seen in Chapter V, such participation tends to be directed to the solution of these narrow problems and is likely to have little impact on other members of the deprived group. And this path to participation operates largely in relation to contacting, a mode of activity to which Blacks and Harijans have least access. External mobilization (or partisan mobilization in the particular form this takes in our analysis) can also bring deprived groups into participation as our data on Harijan voting behavior make clear. But it is uncertain whether such participation will result in the benefit of the participating group. It may, but much depends on the benevolence of those who are doing the mobilization. In the absence of psychological involvement in politics, or information about politics, or a sense of the political relevance of one's group membership—all of which seem to be absent from the process that brings Harijans to the vote—it becomes difficult for members of the deprived group to enforce the use of their participation for their own benefit and not for that of those party leaders who mobilize them.

The group consciousness model, on the other hand, can mobilize members of deprived groups to participate and does so out of an attitudinal framework that ought to lead to demands and pressures for improvement for that group. We can end this book by looking a bit more closely at the consequences of group consciousness. Group consciousness, we have suggested, is more strongly developed among Blacks than among Harijans. Our data support this, as does a more general consideration of the types and intensity of the political movements among the two groups. The difference probably lies in the differences in the absolute socioeconomic levels of the two groups—Harijans have fewer of the skills needed to develop the leadership able to create a sense of group consciousness; they are less connected to each other by mass media that can foster self-awareness. And they are divided from each other by residence in more isolated places, by differences in language, and by subgroup identification.

The different role of group consciousness in the political activity of Blacks and Harijans is illustrated in Figure 14. There we present the rates of regular voting among four groups in each of the countries. The four groups are: the dominant group in each country (whites and caste-Hindus); the deprived group (Blacks and Harijans); and two different types of members of the deprived group—those who do not express a sense of group consciousness and those who do. The latter distinction is based on whether or not a respondent mentioned race or caste in response to a series of open-ended questions about local and national politics, problems, and conflicts. Since we are interested in the difference between the dominant group and the others, we have made the bar representing the activity rate of the dominant group the same length in this figure and in following figures, though the actual rate differs. It makes the comparison easier. The dotted line, also, represents the activity rate of the dominant group. Thus one can clearly see whether some other group is less active, as active, or more active than the dominant group.

The contrast between the situation in the United States and that in India is quite striking when it comes to voting. Consider the data on the United States in Figure 14. They offer an excellent illustration of the role of group consciousness in relation to the participation of Black Americans. The first bar reflects the fact that forty-eight percent of the white sample are regular voters. As the second bar indicates, thirty-eight percent of the Blacks are. What is interesting is the comparison in the next two bars between the Blacks who do not manifest group consciousness and those who do. Only twenty-four percent of the former group are regular voters; forty-six percent of the latter group are—a figure almost identical to that of the whites. In a sense, group consciousness seems to close the gap in activity rate between whites and Blacks; Blacks who are group conscious vote as frequently as do whites; those Blacks who are not group conscious vote less frequently.

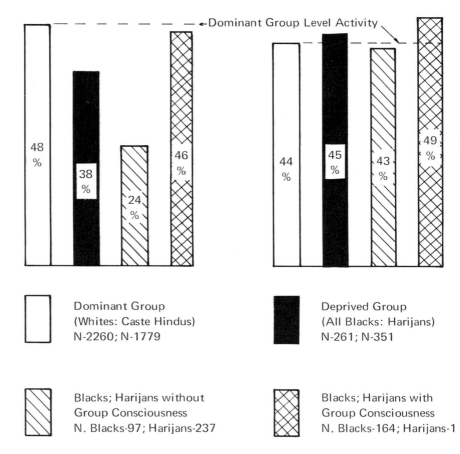

Figure 14
GROUP CONSCIOUSNESS AND VOTING

In India, one finds group consciousness playing no such role in relation to Harijan voting. Harijans are as active as caste-Hindus. And those who manifest no group consciousness are no less active than those who do. Whereas the "group conscious" Black was twice as likely to be a regular voter than the Black without group consciousness, the sense of the political relevance of one's group has no impact on Harijan voting. This is, of course, consistent with the important role of passive partisan mobilization among Harijan voters.

But this does not mean that group consciousness never plays a role among Harijans. As the previous chapter indicated, the group consciousness model does seem to fit the campaign activity of Harijans. And this is reflected in the data on Figure 15—a figure that takes the same form as the previous one, but with frequency of campaign activity substituted for frequency of voting. For both Blacks and Harijans, the sense of group membership plays a role in the frequency of campaign activity. And in each case, group consciousness closes the gap between the dominant and deprived groups. Indeed, the group conscious Blacks or Harijans are more active in campaigns than are whites or caste-Hindus.

On Figure 16, we have the data on cooperative activity. For Blacks, group consciousness again closes the gap between them and the dominant group. For Harijans, the situation is a bit more ambiguous, with some small increase in activity associated with group consciousness.

And Figure 17 reports similar data on frequency of contacting. And here the data are strikingly similar. In relation to contacting—where the gap between deprived and dominant group is greatest in each nation—there is no relationship between group consciousness and activity for Blacks or Harijans. The self-conscious Black is not more likely to contact an official than is the non-self-conscious Black—though the former is more active than the latter in all three other ways. The self-conscious Harijan is no more active than the non-self-conscious one. The difference between contacting and the other activities is consistent with two characteristics of contacting that we mentioned in Chapter V. For one thing, contacting requires that the Black or Harijan contactor in most cases cross an ascriptive barrier between him and the government official. More important may be the fact that, as was

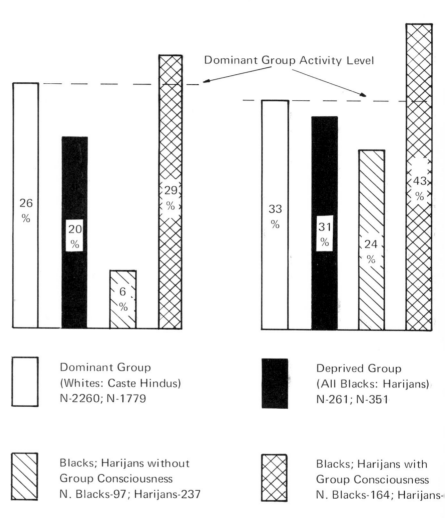

Figure 15

GROUP CONSCIOUSNESS AND CAMPAIGN ACTIVITY

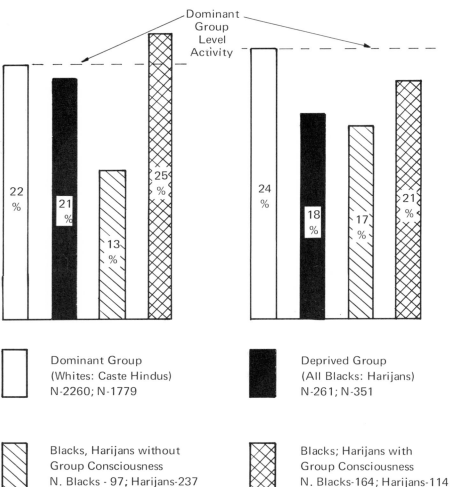

United States   *India*

Frequency of Cooperative Activists

Dominant Group Level Activity

Figure 16

GROUP CONSCIOUSNESS AND COOPERATIVE ACTIVITY

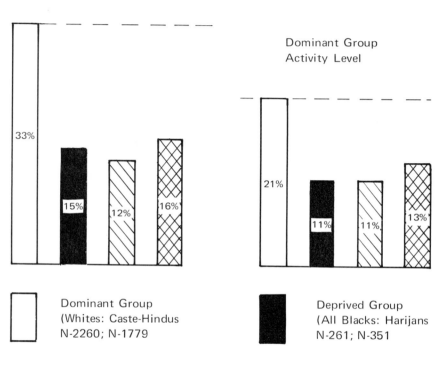

Figure 17
GROUP CONSCIOUSNESS AND CONTACTING

also pointed out in Chapter V, contacting is often for Blacks and Harijans a highly particularistic activity whereby individuals seek benefits for themselves and their families. Insofar as group consciousness affects the political mobilization of the group, it would not be likely to increase such activities.

The data on Figures 14 through 17 illustrate the consequences of the group consciousness model presented in the previous chapter. The model "works" to the benefit of Blacks in three out of the four modes of activity. Blacks are on the average much lower on such socioeconomic measures as education, income, and occupation. But where they have developed group consciousness, their participation moves to a level higher than one would have predicted on the basis of those socioeconomic characteristics alone. Nor is the situation merely a reflection of a higher social status of the group conscious Blacks in contrast to other Blacks. The two groups differ little in socioeconomic status. Indeed, if one controls for the socioeconomic level of the Blacks, one would find the group conscious Blacks participating at a rate well above that of their white counterparts (see Verba and Nie, forthcoming).

For Harijans, one sees some evidence of the impact of group consciousness, but the evidence of impact is less. Where large proportions of Harijans are mobilized—as in voting—group consciousness plays little role. Only in relation to campaign activity does group consciousness seem to be important. And even there—where the difference between group conscious Harijans and others is great—we must remember one other fact about the difference between Blacks and Harijans in the importance of group consciousness. The proportion of Harijans who can be characterized as group conscious is much smaller than the proportion of Blacks who can be so characterized. Using the more inclusive measure of group consciousness we have employed, which gives the respondent more chances to mention his group, we classify sixty-three percent of our Black sample as conscious of the political relevance of their group in comparison with thirty-two percent of the Harijans. Thus, even where group consciousness increases the activity rate of the Harijan who has developed that consciousness, its impact on the overall activity rate of the group is limited by the fact that a small proportion of the Harijans have this sense of the political relevance of group membership.

In some sense, we may be seeing early traces of the working of the group consciousness model among Harijans, a model that would work with greater potency if the sense of self-awareness were to grow.

SOME CONCLUSIONS

We began this book with a concern with the question of the ways in which deprived groups could use the political system to overcome their deprivation. The comparison between Blacks in the United States and Harijans in India was, we argued, interesting because of a series of similarities and differences between the groups and between the social settings in which they lived. And we argued that though there was no question that Blacks and Harijans could be compared—anything can be compared with anything—the more meaningful question was whether the comparison was fruitful, whether it gave us greater insight into the problems of each of the groups, as well as greater insight into some of the more general problems relating to the politics of deprivation. We hope that our book has demonstrated the fruitfulness of such comparison for both the understanding of the particular groups and for understanding the more general problem as well.

The data on the ways in which the two deprived groups participate do fit our expectations based on the combination of similarities and differences between the groups. It may be useful to summarize a few of these:

(1) If deprived groups are to use political mechanisms as a means of advance in the socioeconomic sphere, the political system must be more open to them than the socioeconomic system. Our consideration of the dominant ideologies and institutional structures in the two countries led us to expect that in fact there would be more equalitarian access to the political than to the socioeconomic system. And we found this to be the case. Looked at relative to the dominant group in each country, Blacks and Harijans are less deprived in terms of political participation than in terms of socioeconomic status. And both groups have better access to advancement via government than via private employ. In this sense, the two groups are similar.

(2) And the ways in which Blacks and Harijans participate in politics are similar also. In particular, the ascriptive barriers separating them from the dominant groups—and from the government officials who are largely of the dominant group—leads to the large differences between the deprived and dominant groups in terms of their access to the government via citizen-initiated contacts.

(3) But some differences in the conditions of the two groups lead to differences in their political behavior. The two major differences between the groups are the lower absolute socio-economic level of Harijans compared with Blacks and the greater internal heterogeneity among Harijans in terms of language and subgroup affiliations. We expected these differences to reduce the ability of the Harijans to organize themselves for political action.

(4) This expectation was supported both by the data on the rate and kind of activity engaged in by these two groups and by the differences in the processes by which they appear to come to participate. Blacks were particularly active in cooperative modes of participation and were in fact as active as whites in such participation. Harijans matched the participation rates of caste-Hindus in voting, but not in cooperative activity.

(5) And while a sense of group consciousness seems to be crucial in bringing Blacks into participation, the path to participation for Harijans—particularly when it comes to voting—is largely one of external mobilization involving an important role for partisan attachment. However, though fewer Harijans seem to be conscious of the political relevance of their group membership, we did find an instance where—in relation to campaign activity—such an orientation was bringing Harijans into political participation.

We have in this volume greatly complicated the analysis of political mobilization from what one often finds in the literature. In much previous work, the aim has been to find the best-fitting path model to political participation across all kinds of political acts and across all population groups. We have, in contrast, looked at alternative paths to participation—different paths to different kinds of activity for different groups. We believe this complexity is necessary, since the modes of activity differ systematically in how they relate the citizen to his government and since the ways in which different groups come to participate may differ. But we do not want to move to such a low level of generality where all we can say is that for this particular group this seems to be the path to this type of participation. Rather, we believe that there are some general characteristics of groups and of acts that make it likely that certain types of groups will come to participate in particular ways through particular paths. Thus the difference between Harijans and Blacks in terms of the greater potency of group consciousness on the part of the latter and the greater importance of the partisan mobilized model among the former derives, we believe, from the lower availability to Harijans of skilled leadership and communications facilities, as well as their greater dispersion.

In some sense, this volume can have no conclusion, and this for two reasons. In the first place, the intellectual questions raised need further exploration. More complex models of the ways in which citizens come to participate should be tested. We have, for instance, paid little attention to the role of voluntary organizations, to the community context of the participating citizen. And we can, within these two countries, expand our frame of reference to include other groups in the society. Furthermore, many of the questions asked can be asked across more countries—the politics of deprivation exists in most places. These analyses, involving an expansion of the framework used in this book, will be attempted in future publications of the research project from which the material in this book was drawn (see note 1, Chapter I). In this volume, we have isolated a particular problem—the political behavior of two most interesting and important parallel groups. This analysis may be thought of as a preliminary to a more general analysis of the politics of deprivation and, more generally still, of the politics of participation.

Secondly, this volume can have no conclusion, since the particular problem we study has no conclusion. We have seen a snapshot of the political activities of two severely deprived groups. And that snapshot shows some of the dynamic forces affecting Black and Harijan political activity. But where those developments lead and when and how the struggle for equality ends—if it ever does—are questions whose answers lie in the future. The answers depend on the response of the dominant groups and they depend on the activity of the deprived groups.

APPENDICES

APPENDIX A

SURVEY DESIGN

The data reported in this monograph come from a larger study of political participation and political development in India and the United States, as well as in several other countries. The samples have, therefore, some special features somewhat irrelevant to the problems dealt with here. The sampels were designed to accomplish three not completely compatible goals: estimates of characteristics of the population from which sample was drawn (the adult United States population and the adult population in four Indian states—Uttar Pradesh, Andhra Pradesh, West Bengal, and Gujarat); relationships between characteristics of the population and characteristics of the communities within which they live (for which purpose there was oversampling in some communities where interviews were also conducted with local leaders and community information gathered); and comparisons across the societies studied (for which purpose the nonurban segments of the United States sample were increased while the urban segment of the Indian data was increased). In data analyses the samples were reweighted. Fuller descriptions of the samples in each nation will be contained in forthcoming monographs devoted to each of the nations. The following is a brief summary.

United States: The sample was based on one regularly used by the National Opinion Research Center of the University of Chicago for its amalgam surveys. This is a standard multistage area probability sample to the block or segment level. At the block level, however, quota sampling is used with quotas based on sex, age, race, and employment status. Though sampling error cannot be computed directly because of the quota characteristic, experience with the sample allows estimates of variability which suggest that the sample has the same efficiency as a simple random sample about two-thirds the size of the NORC sample—that is, a sample of 1,500 has the efficiency of a simple random sample of 1,000. The quota nature of the sample does not allow the report of response rates.

In our study, we tripled the size of the sample taken from that one-third of the universe living in communities under 50,000 in population. In analyzing the data, the sample was appropriately weighted.

India: The Indian sample was limited to four states (because of the administrative costs of conducting the study in too many linguistic areas and because of a desire to compare subcultures within India). The four states were selected purposefully to represent the four regional groupings in India. The four states were Uttar Pradesh, Andhra Pradesh, West Bengal, and Gujarat.

The sample in each state was divided into a rural sample (places under 10,000 in population) and an urban sample of towns and cities. The urban sample was increased in size by a factor of 3. In addition, it was decided to undersample women in both urban and rural areas: in rural areas by a factor of 4, in urban areas by a factor of 2½. In analyzing the data, the sample was appropriately weighted.

In the rural sample, a multistage probability selection was made to the village level using the district and the block as the intervening stages. Districts were stratified according to their development levels (using the Pal-Subramaniam index developed at the Indian Statistical Institute, Calcutta), blocks by distance to district headquarters, and villages by size. Districts and blocks were selected with probability proportional to size. Within blocks, villages were selected from two size strata with equal probability and the quota of interviews for the block divided among the villages proportional to the size of the villages.

In the urban samples, towns and cities were randomly selected from three strata and interviews allocated within them proportional to the size of the stratum. One stratum contained the state capitals which were always selected, and the other two strata were based on size. In larger cities (over 50,000), a similar procedure was used for the selection of wards.

Respondents were chosen randomly from official lists of eligible voters maintained both for urban areas and villages. These lists are revised from time to time—more frequently in rural than in urban areas. But the urban lists had been revised and updated shortly before our field work in preparation for the national elections in 1967.

The response rate was eighty percent with a range between seventy-seven percent and ninety percent across the four states.

APPENDIX B

QUESTIONS, SCALES AND INDICES
USED IN THE UNITED STATES STUDY

Exposure to Mass Media of Communication

Item:

(1) How often do you watch the news broadcast on television—every day, a few hours a week, about once a week, or never?

(2) How often do you read the newspaper—every day, a few times a week, about once a week, or never?

(3) How often do you read magazines—every day, a few times a week, about once a week, or never?

The person who had no exposure to any of the above mass media was given the value (0); the person who was exposed to only one of the three was given the value (1); those who were exposed to two of the mass media were given the value (2); those exposed to all three were given the highest value (3).

Political Interests

Item:

(1) In general, how often do you discuss politics and national affairs with others—every day, maybe once or twice a week, less than once a week, or never?

(2) How interested are you in politics and national affairs—are you very interested, somewhat interested, only slightly interested, or not at all interested?

(3) How often do you discuss local community problems with others in this community—every day, at least once a week, or less than once a week?

This was a simple additive scale where the persons who replied in the negative (never) were given the lowest value (0), and the persons who answered positively on all three items were given the highest value (3).

Political Information

Item:

(1) We are interested in how well known the community leaders are in different places—what is the name of the [mention position title of the head of the local government unit] of one's community?
(2) What is the name of the head of the local school system?
(3) How old does a person have to be in order to vote in his state?
(4) We want to know how well the different governmental leaders are known around here—could you tell me the name of the governor of this state?
(5) And what are the names of the senators from this state?
(6) What about the congressman from this district—do you happen to know his name?
(7) What is the name of your state capital?

The information scale was a simple additive scale of the number of correct answers.

Partisanship

Item:

(1) Generally speaking, do you usually think of yourself as a Republican, a Democrat, an Independent, or what?

(2) If Democrat or Republican—would you call yourself a strong (Republican/Democrat), or not a very strong (Republican/Democrat)?

(3) If Independent, no party, other, or don't know—do you consider yourself as closer to the Republican or Democratic Party?

The person who replied that he did not think of himself as either Democrat or Republican nor did he consider himself to be closer to any Party was given the lowest value and considered nonpartisan. Those who did not consider themselves Democrat or Republican but considered themselves closer to either of the two parties were called "weak partisans." Those who considered themselves strong supporters were rated as "moderate partisans," and those who were strong supporters were rated as "strong partisans."

Government as Solver of Personal Problems

Item:

(This item was asked as a follow-up question to a question about the most important personal problem the individual had. It was asked of each problem mentioned.)

(1) Who is most able to help you with that [respondent's personal] problem?

The respondents were divided into two categories. Those who mentioned government as a solver of personal problems and those who did not mention government, in response to the above question.

Group Consciousness

Item:

(1) In many communities there are groups that are opposed to each other. Thinking still about this community

(mention name of local government unit), what are the major groups that oppose each other here?

(2) When you think of your own situation and that of your family what are the problems that concern you most?

(3) What is the most important problem in this community?

(4) So far we have been talking about the local community. Now think about the country as a whole. What are the most important problems facing the United States today?

The group consciousness score was based on the frequency with which respondents mentioned race or racial problems in response to the above items. The data in Table 17 (Chapter 4) are based on the first item alone. Elsewhere the more inclusive measure is used.

Voting

Item:

(1) Can you tell me how you voted in the 1964 Presidential election—did you vote for Johnson or Goldwater or perhaps you did not vote?

(2) And how about in 1960—can you tell me how you voted in the Presidential election—did you vote for Kennedy or Nixon or perhaps you did not vote?

(3) What about local elections—do you always vote in those, do you sometimes miss one, or do you rarely vote, or do you never vote?

Those who did not vote in any of the presidential elections or local elections were given the lowest value (0) as "nonvoters." Those who voted in one of the presidential elections or local elections were given the value (1) as "occasional voters" and those who voted in both the presidential elections and always voted in local elections were given the highest value (2) as "regular voters."

Participation in Campaign and Party Activities

Item:

(1) During elections do you ever try to show people why they should vote for one of the parties of candidates—do you most often, sometimes, rarely, or never?

(2) Have you ever done work for one of the parties or candidates in most elections, some elections, only a few, or have you never done such work?

(3) In the past three or four years have you attended any political meetings or rallies—[if yes] about how many times?

(4) Membership in political groups or organizations.

Those who reported as not active in response to any of the four questions were given the value (0); those who reported active in response to one or two of the above questions were given the value of (1) as "somewhat active"; and those who reported active in response to all the questions were given the value (2) as "very active."

Participation in Cooperative Activities

Item:

(1) Have you ever worked with others in this community to try to solve some community problem?

(2) Have you ever taken part in forming a new group or a new organization to try to solve some community problem?

(3) Active membership in any organization the respondent reports as itself active in community affairs—based on a set of questions on organizational affiliation, activity, and description of these organizations.

Those who had not engaged in any of the above activities were given the lowest value (0); those who did one of the two activities were given the value (1) as "somewhat active"; and those who engaged in more than one of the activities were given the highest value (2) as "very active."

Contacting Elites

Item:

(1) We were talking about problems that you and the people of this community have—have you ever personally gone to see or spoken to or written to some member of the local government or some other person of influence in the community about some need or problem?

(2) How about some representative or governmental official outside the local community—have you ever contacted or written to such a person on some need or problem?

Those who contacted neither a local elite nor an elite outside the community were rated as having "no contacts," while those who had either contacted local elite or external elite or both were rated as having "contacts."

Perceived Ability to Contact the Elite Directly

Item:

(1) Suppose you had some problem to take up with an important official in the local government, such as the mayor or some local councilman, but you did not personally know this official—would it be necessary to go through some connections to approach this official or could you approach him directly?

The values given were as follows: (0) connections necessary to contact elite; (1) depends; (2) can contact directly.

Easy Availability of Connections for Contacting Elite

Item:

(1) [For those who need connections], if such a situation arose, could you easily find some such person who could help you make such a contact?

Following were the values given: (0) cannot find connections; (1) may find connections; (2) can easily find connections.

Socioeconomic Status of Family

Item:

(1) Family income
(2) Education of the head of the household.
(3) Occupation of the head of the household.
(4) Scale of material possesions (such as credit card, charge account, or checking account).

The items were standardized into Z scores and added up. The standardized SES variable then was recoded into approximately six equal parts.

Overall Participation Scale

To build a general index of participation with continuous values, we used the result of a factor analysis of all participation variables. First, orthogonal factor scales were built for each dimension, there the overall scale was built by combining the factor scores on each dimension. For certain analysis, the overall participation scale that was originally continuous was then collapsed into six approximately equal categories.

APPENDIX C

QUESTIONS, SCALES AND INDICES USED IN INDIA

Exposure to Mass Media of Communications

Item:

(1) Do you ever read the newspaper or have someone read it out to you—about how often?

(2) Do you ever go to the cinema?

(3) Do you ever listen to the radio?

Those who were not exposed to any of the three media were given the value (0); those who either read the newspaper, went to see a movie, or listened to the radio were given the value (1); those who were exposed to two of three media were given the value (2); and those who were exposed to all the three media were given the value (3).

Political Interest

Item:

(1) In general, how often do you discuss politics and national affairs with others—every day, maybe once or twice a week, less than once a week, or never?

(2) How interested are you in politics and national affairs—are you very interested, somewhat interested, only slightly interested, or not at all interested?

(3) How often do you discuss local community problems with others in this community—every day, at least once a week, or less than once a week?

This was a simple additive scale where the persons who replied in the negative (never) were given the lowest value (0), and the persons who answered positively on all three items were given the highest value (3).

Political Information

Item:

(1) How old does a person have to be in order to vote?
(2) Do you know who is our Prime Minister?
(3) And who is the Chief Minister of the State?
(4) To which party does the Chief Minister belong?
(5) Will you please name the main opposition party in the state legislature?

The number of correct answers was summed.

Partisanship

Item:

(1) Which party do you support?
(2) [For those who support a party] Do you consider yourself a strong supporter of that party?
(3) [For those who said they do not support a party] If you had to choose, is there any party that you might prefer?

A person who replied he did not think of himself as supporting any party and who did not mention a party when asked what he would do if he had to choose was given the lowest value and considered "nonpartisan." Those who did not support a party but mentioned a party on the follow-up question were considered "weak partisans." Those who reported that they supported a party but said they were not strong supporters were rated "moderate partisans." And those who considered themselves strong supporters were rated "strong partisans."

Government as Solver of Personal Problems

    Item:

(This item was asked as a follow-up question to a question about the most important personal problem the individual had. It was asked of each problem mentioned.)

    (1) Who is most able to help you with that [respondent's personal] problem?

The respondents were divided into two categories. Those who mentioned government as a solver of personal problems and those who did not mention government, in response to the above question.

Group Consciousness

    Same as in the United States with the addition of the following item:

    Which groups or organizations are most influential in the affairs of this village/town?

The group consciousness score was based on frequency of mention of caste or caste problems in response to the various open questions. The data in Table 17 (Chapter IV) are based on the item on "opposing groups" (see United States item list) alone. Elsewhere the more inclusive measure is used.

Voting

    Item:

    (1) How often have you voted in the national elections—have you voted every time, most of the time, or rarely?

(2) How often have you voted in Panchayat/Municipal elections—have you voted every time, most of the time, or rarely?

Those who did not vote in either of the two elections were rated "nonvoters." Those who occasionally voted in national and local elections were rated "occasional voters." And those who voted regularly in both local and national elections were rated "regular voters."

Participation in Campaign and Party Activities

Item:

(1) Are you a member of any political party?

(2) Have you given money for a political cause?

(3) Have you ever attended a political meeting or rally during an election or at any other time? [If yes] About how many times?

(4) Have you ever engaged in any activity during a political campaign to elect some candidates?

Those who reported themselves as not active in response to any of the four questions were given the value (0); those who reported active in response to one or two of the above questions were given the value (1) as "somewhat active"; and those who reported active in response to three or more questions were given the value (2) as "very active."

Participation in Cooperative Activities

Item:

(1) Have you ever worked with others in this community to try to solve some community problem?

(2) Have you ever taken part in forming a new group or a new organization to try to solve some community problem?

(3) Active membership in any organization the respondent reports as itself active in community affairs—based on a set of

questions on organizational affiliation, activity, and description of these organizations.

Those who had not engaged in any of the above activities were given the lowest value (0); those who did one of the two activities were given the value (1) as "somewhat active"; and those who engaged in more than one of the activities were given the highest value (2) as "very active."

Contacting Elite

Item:

(1) Have you ever personally contacted—I mean gone to see or spoken to or written to some member of the Panchayat/Municipality or some other person of influence in the village/town about some need or problem? [if yes] Who?

(2) What about some representative or government official at block/district/state level? Have you ever contacted or perhaps written to such a person on some need or problem? At which level? What was his position?

Those who contacted neither any local elite nor elite outside the community were rated as having "no contacts," while those who had either contacted local elite or external elite or both were rated as having "contacts."

Perceived Ability to Contact the Elite Directly

Item:

(1) Suppose you had some problem to take up with an important official in this village/town such as V.L.W/ Municipal Tax collector or Sanitary Inspector, but you did not personally know this officer, would it be necessary to go through some personal connections to approach the official or could you approach him directly?

The values given were as follows: (0) connections necessary to contact elite; (1) depends; (2) can contact directly.

Availability of Connections for Contacting Elite

Item:

(1) [For those who need connections], if such a situation arose, could you easily find some such person who could help you make such a contact?

Following were the values given: (0) cannot find connections; (1) may find connections; (2) can easily find connections.

Socioeconomic Status

Item:

(1) Family income.
(2) Education of the head of the household.
(3) Occupation of the head of the household.
(4) Scale of material possessions (such as radio, savings account, watch, conveyance, table and chair).

The items were standardized into Z scores and added up. The standardized SES variable then was recoded into approximately six equal parts.

Overall Participation Scale

Same as in the United States except that one scale with voting and one without voting are used.

REFERENCES

REFERENCES

AMBEDKAR, B. R. (1945) What Congress and Gandhi Have Done to the Untouchables. Bombay: Thacker.

BAILEY, F. G. (1963) "Closed social stratification in India." Archives of European Sociology 4, 1: 107-124.

—— (1959) "For a sociology of India." Contributions to Indian Sociology 3 (July): 88-101.

BERREMAN, GERALD D. (1966) "Structure and functions of the caste system," in G. de Vos and H. Wagatsama, Japan's Invisible Race: Caste in Culture and Personality. Berkeley: Univeristy of California Press.

—— (1960) "Caste in India and the United States." Amer. J. of Sociology 66 (September): 120-127.

BETTEILLE, ANDRE (1965) "Future of the backward classes." A special supplement of the Indian Journal of Public Administration 11 (January-March).

BHATT, ANIL (1969) "Social mobility and politics in India." (forthcoming)

—— (1963) "Caste and politics in Akola." Economic Weekly (August 24).

BLAU, PETER and O. D. DUNCAN (1967) The American Occupational Structure. New York: John Wiley.

CASH, W. J. (1954) The Mind of the South. Garden City, N.Y.: Doubleday.

COATMAN, JOHN (1933) "Reforms in India and the depressed classes." Asiatic Review (January): 46.

Commission for Scheduled Castes and Scheduled Tribes (n.d.) Report, 1960-61. Statistical Appendix 44. Part II. New Delhi: Government of India.

COX, OLIVER C. (1945) "Race and caste: a distinction." American Journal of Sociology 50 (March): 360-368.

DALTON, DENNIS (1967) "The Gandhian view of caste and caste after Gandhi," pp. 159-191 in P. Mason (ed.) India and Ceylon: Unity and Diversity. London: Oxford University Press.

DOLBEER, MARTIN LUTHER (1929) "The movement for the emancipation of Untouchable classes in South India." Master's thesis. University of Chicago.

DOLLARD, JOHN (1957) Caste and Class in a Southern Town. New York: Doubleday.

DUMONT, LOUIS (1961) "Caste, racism and 'stratification,' reflections of a social anthropologist." Contributions to Indian Sociology 5 (November-October): 21-43.

—— and D. POCOCK (1957) "For a sociology of India." Contributions to Indian Sociology 1 (November): 7-22.

DUSHKIN, LELAH (1961) "Removal of disabilities—legal and other provisions." Economic Weekly (November 4): 1697-1705.

ESSEIN-UDOM, E. U. (1962) Black Nationalism: A Search for Identity in America. Chicago: Dell.

FRANKLIN, JOHN HOPE (1969) From Slavery to Freedom: A History of American Negroes. New York: Vintage.

GALANTER, MARC (1969) "Untouchability and the law." Economic and Political Weekly, Annual 1 (January): 131-170.

—— (1963) "Law and caste in modern India." Asian Survey 3 (November): 544-559.

—— (1961a) "Equality and 'protective discrimination' in India." Rutgers Law Review 16 (Fall): 42-74.

—— (1961b) "Protective discrimination for backward classes in India." Journal of the Indian Law Institute (January-March).

HEIMSATH, CHARLES (1964) Indian Nationalism and Hindu Social Reform. Princeton: Princeton Univ. Press.

IRSCHICK, EUGENE F. (1969) Politics and Social Conflict in South India. Berkeley and Los Angeles: University of California Press.

ISAACS, HAROLD R. (1964) India's Ex-Untouchables. New York: John Day.

JANS, J., S.J. (1935) The Depressed Classes—A Chronological Documentation. Volume 1. Ranchi: Catholic Press.

KEER, DHANANJEY (1962) Dr. Ambedkar—Life and Mission. Bombay: Popular Prakashan.

LEACH, E. R. (1960) "Introduction: what should we mean by caste," pp. 1-10 in E. R. Leach (ed.) Aspects of Caste in South India, Ceylon, and Northwest Pakistan. Cambridge Papers in Social Anthropology. Cambridge, Eng.: Cambridge University Press.

LINCOLN, C. ERIC (1961) The Black Muslim in America. Boston: Beacon Press.

LOMAX, LOUIS (1962) The Negro Revolt. New York: New American Library.

LYNCH, OWEN (1968) "Politics of Untouchability," in M. Singer and B. Cohn (eds.) Social Structure and Change in India. Chicago: Aldine.

MYRDAL, GUNNAR (1944) An American Dilemma. New York: Harper.

NATARAJAN, S. (1959) A Century of Social Reform in India. London: Asia Publishing.

NEHRU, RAMESHWARI (1950) The Harijan Movement. Delhi: Harijan Sevak Sangh.

NIE, NORMAN, G. B. POWELL, Jr., and KENNETH PREWITT (1969) "Social structure and political participation: developmental relationships." American Political Science Review (June and September): 361-378 and 808-832.

NURULLAH, S. and J. P. NAIK (1951) History of Education. Bombay: Macmillan.

OLSEN, MARVIN E. (1970) "Social and political participation of Blacks." American Sociological Review 35: 682-696.

PYARELAL, U. N. (1932) The Epic Fast. Ahmedahad: Mohanlal Maganlal Bhatt.

de REUCK, ANTHONY and JULIE KNIGHT [eds.] (1967) Caste and Race: Comparative Approaches. Boston: Little, Brown.

ROSE, ARNOLD M. [ed.] (1964) Assuring Freedom to the Free. Detroit: Wayne State University Press.

RUDOLPH, LLOYD I. and SUZANNE H. RUDOLPH (1967) The Modernity of Tradition. Chicago: University of Chicago Press.

SCHUMAN, HAROLD (1969) "Sociological racism." Trans-action 7 (December): 44-48.

SINHA, SURAJIT (1967) "Caste in India: its essential patterns of socio-cultural integration," in A. de Reuck and J. Knight (eds.) Caste and Race: Comparative Approaches. Boston: Little, Brown.

SRINIVAS, M. N. (1968) "Mobility in the caste system," pp. 189-200 in M. Singer and B. Cohn (eds.) Structure and Change in Indian Society. Chicago: Aldine.

—— (1966) Social Change in Modern India. Bombay: Allied Publishers.

—— (1962) Caste in Modern India and Other Essays. Bombay: Asia Publishing.

TINKER, HUGH (1962) India and Pakistan—A Political Analysis. New York: Frederick A. Praeger.

VERBA, SIDNEY (1969) "Survey research and comparative politics," in S. Rokkan, J. Viet, and E. Almasy (eds.) Comparative Survey Analysis. Paris: The Hague, Monbon.

—— and NORMAN H. NIE (forthcoming) Participation in American Political Life. New York: Harper & Row.

——NORMAN H. NIE and JAE-ON KIM (1971) "Modes of political participation." Sage Professional Papers in Comparative Politics. Volume 2. Series Number 01-013.

de VOS, GEORGE and HIROSHI WAGATSUMA (1966) Japan's Invisible Race: Caste in Culture and Personality. Berkeley: University of California Press.

WILSON, JAMES Q. (1964) "The changing political position of the Negro,"
     pp. 163-184 in A. M. Rose (ed.) Assuring Freedom to the Free. Detroit:
     Wayne State University Press.
—— (1960) Negro Politics: The Search for Leadership. Glencoe: Free Press.
ZELLIOTT, ELEANOR (1969) "Dr. Ambedkar and the Mahar movement."
     Ph.D. dissertation. University of Pennsylvania.
—— (1966) "Buddhism and politics in Maharashtra," in D. Smith (ed.) South
     Asian Politics and Religion. Princeton: Princeton Univ. Press.

ABOUT THE AUTHORS

SIDNEY VERBA is Professor of Political Science at the University of Chicago and Senior Study Director at the National Opinion Research Center of that University. He formerly taught at Princeton and Stanford Universities. He is the author of *Small Groups and Political Behavior* (Princeton, 1961) and the co-author of *The Civic Culture* (Princeton, 1963); of *Political Culture and Political Development* (Princeton, 1965); and of *Comparative Survey Analysis* (Mouton, 1969).

BASHIRUDDIN AHMED has taught political science at Osmania University in India and is currently a Research Fellow of the Centre for the Study of Developing Societies, New Delhi. He has conducted regional and national studies of political behavior in India and has contributed to scholarly journals in these topics.

ANIL BHATT is a Research Associate of the Centre for the Study of Developing Societies in New Delhi. He is currently involved in a study of the role of caste in politics in India, and has published articles on this subject.

INDEX

INDEX

Constitution—India, 62
Contacting—group consciousness and, 235
Cooperative activity—group consciousness and, 235
Courts—use by Blacks, 66
      use by Harijan, 47, 66
Cox, Oliver—17

Dalton, Dennis—58
Democratic Party—71, 111
Depressed Classes Institute—52, 66
Depressed Class Mission Society of India—50
Dolbeer, Martin Luther—52
Dollard, John — 16, 17
DuBois, W.E.B.—66
Dumont, Louis—17, 21
Duncan, O.D.—187
Dushkin, Lelah—62

Education—33
      Blacks and Harijans compared, 84-89
      British reforms, 44-45
      and participation, 164-173
Elphinstone, Montstuart—44
Essein-Udom, E.U.—70

Franklin, John Hope—65
Freedmen's Aid Society—67

Galanter, Marc—47, 55, 62, 188
Gandhi, Indira—64
Gandhi Mohandas K.—50, 53, 54, 56, 58, 70
Garvey, Marcus—70
Government of India Act of 1919—50
Great Britain—rule in India, 44-46
Group consciousness—25, 26, 113-116, 147-149, 204, 210, 215, 220, 231-243
      and campaign activity, 235
      and contacting, 235
      and cooperative activity, 235
      and voting, 233

Harijans—history of, 42-65
      origin of term, 56